I and II THESSALONIANS
The Prospect of Glory

John L. Benson

". . . he called you by our
gospel to the obtaining
of the glory of our
Lord Jesus Christ."

–II Thessalonians 2:14

ACCENT ON LIFE
BIBLE CURRICULUM

ADULT STUDENT
Bible Study Guide

This Bible Study Guide is part of a ten-year adult curriculum designed to assist you in making the entire Bible your Guide for daily living.

John L. Benson/Author
James T. Dyet/Executive Editor
Robert L. Mosier/Publisher

Accent on Life Bible Curriculum
Accent-B/P Publications
12100 W. Sixth Avenue
P.O. Box 15337
Denver, Colorado 80215

ISBN 0-89636-061-X

I and II THESSALONIANS

The Prospect of Glory

John L. Benson

CONTENTS

THE BEGINNING OF A GREAT CHURCH

1

LESSON SCRIPTURE
Acts 15:36—17:10

RELATED SCRIPTURE
The Book of Philippians

LESSON AIM
To take the gospel to at least one person this week; to pray daily for missionary personnel and projects.

LEARN BY HEART
"For our gospel came not unto you in word only, but also in power, and in the Holy Ghost, and in much assurance; as ye know what manner of men we were among you for your sake (I Thessalonians 1:5).

EVERY DAY WITH THE WORD

STUDENT'S NOTEBOOK

This column is for the student who desires additional study of the lesson theme.

Monday	A message of life	Acts 3:12-26
Tuesday	A message of peace	Acts 10:34-43
Wednesday	A message of joy	Acts 13:26-41
Thursday	A message of grace	Acts 14:1-5
Friday	A message of hope	Acts 23:6-11
Saturday	A message of liberty	II Corinthians 3:1-18
Sunday	A message of light	II Corinthians 4:1-7

LESSON PREPARATION

Opportunity never comes— it's here.

An old Japanese saying suggests that two kinds of opportunities are possible: the kind we chance upon, and the kind we create. Either kind may represent the opportunity of a lifetime, but we are far more likely to recognize and take advantage of the opportunities which we create.

This attitude motivated Paul to take the initiative and start out on a second missionary expedition. He did not wait until opportunity came knocking at his door. His great pastor's heart impelled him to feel concern for the churches which he had earlier established. He determined to pay them a visit in order to see that they were properly organized and functioning (Acts 15:36).

THE CITIES ON ROUTE TO THE THESSALONIANS

In the company of Silas, Paul took the land route from the city of Antioch, passed through North Syria, and crossed Mount Amanus through the Syrian Gates into Cilicia (Acts 15:41). It was natural that Paul should move in this direction. It was his hometown territory, and possibly he had been evangelizing here for about eight years before Barnabas arrived to bring Paul back to Antioch.

Leaving the coastal plain, the evangelistic team set out for the high country, crossed the Taurus Mountains through the Cilician Gates, and from the summit of the Taurus must have seen the fertile plain of Lycaonia. Another ten days or so would bring them to Derbe, a frontier Roman town on the border of the province of Galatia (Acts 16:1). Their next stop was Lystra, a Roman colony. This city holds the distinction of being the home of Timothy, although he is also associated with Iconium (verse 2). Lystra is situated about 25 miles south of Konya. Adding Timothy to the party, Paul visited the cities of Iconium and Pisidian Antioch (verse 4), confirming the churches that

No doubt Paul wanted to communicate the results of the council of Acts 15 to the brethren.

Barnabas returned to his native land, Cyprus (Acts 15:39), and Paul went to Tarsus, his place of birth. Neither would neglect his home environment.

Derbe has been identified with a large mound at Kerti Huyuk, 65 miles south of modern Konya. Neither Derbe nor Lystra has been excavated.

had sprung up during his first visit to these regions.

Luke tells us that the evangelists next traveled "throughout Phrygia" (verse 6). This district included the towns of Colosse, Hierapolis, and Laodicea. Then we learn that they visited the "region of Galatia." Archaeological discoveries have proved that Antioch in Pisidia, Iconium, Lystra, and Derbe were located in South Galatia, and certainly the Galatian epistle was sent to these churches. It is by no means certain that Paul and his companions visited North Galatia at this time, but if they did, they probably toured the region of modern Ankara, for ancient Ancyra was the chief city of North Galatia.

For some reason the Holy Spirit would not permit Paul and his team to venture into proconsular Asia or the province of Bithynia where stood the inviting cities of Nicaea, Nicomedia, and Chalcedon (verses 6,7). At this point the itinerant missionaries knew only what they must not do, but they had no knowledge of what they should do. Passing alongside Mysia, they finally came to Troas, where they waited for some explicit orders. They knew that a closed door did not mean an end to their labors.

The cities of Troy, Assos, Troas, and Adramyttium were within the borders of Mysia.

Divine direction was not long in coming. In a vision Paul received an SOS from a man of Macedonia (verse 9). This unusual communication convinced Paul that the time had come for him to take another stride—an incursion into Europe. Dr. Luke, a Greek, had joined the company by this time. Perhaps he had been urging Paul to visit Philippi with the message of the gospel, and the vision confirmed what the will of God was in the decision.

In verse 10, note the change of "they" to "we." This indicates that Dr. Luke was with them.

The quartet booked passage aboard a ship and set out to cross the Aegean Sea. They remained the first night on Samothracia and disembarked at Neapolis on the following day (verse 11). Neapolis (modern Kavalla) was a typical harbor town whose inhabitants consisted of a motley array of languages and races. Nothing warranted a delay in Neapolis, and so the evangelists went directly to Philippi (verse 12). Philippi was the seat of medicine and likely attracted Luke to establish his practice there. It was a strategic spot to found a church, for the city was situated near the arteries of trade, culture, and defense. As a Roman colony, it was a replica of Rome. The town boasted of a generous populace of the Roman military and aristocracy.

Probably there was no Jewish community at Neapolis. "Neapolis" means "New City." It served as a port for Philippi.

A clash with heathenism necessitated Paul's departure from Philippi. Leaving Luke behind and taking the Via Egnatia, Paul, Silas, and Timothy passed through Amphipolis and Apollonia (Acts 17:1). They probably remained overnight in these towns, but evidently Paul considered them unimportant in his scheme of evangelization. Thessalonica was the next strategic political and commercial center, and to it the Lord directed their steps.

THE CIRCUMSTANCES OF REACHING THE THESSALONIANS

In keeping with Paul's methodology to preach the gospel to the Jews first and then to the Gentiles, he began his ministry at Thessalonica in the Jewish synagogue (Acts 17:1,2). Here he would find a people who were already conditioned by a long acquaintance with the Old Testament Scrip-

Note Paul's policy in Romans 1:16. "To the Jew first" was never intended to be the procedure for the entire church age. Jews have no more priority than the Gentiles.

Paul remained long enough in the city to necessitate his taking manual labor (I Thessalonians 2:9) and accepting money from the church at Philippi (Philippians 4:16).

tures. Here he would meet Gentiles who had become disillusioned by heathen polytheism and had embraced the faith of Abraham.

If Paul arrived at Thessalonica early in the week, we can imagine how impatiently he waited for Saturday to come. On the Sabbath day he entered the synagogue and began a series of meetings in which he put forth the thesis that Jesus of Nazareth was Israel's Messiah. According to verse 2, the campaign lasted for three Sabbaths—two weeks. Whether this means that Paul's total visit was two weeks or whether it means that his meetings continued two weeks we do not know.

The Jews at Thessalonica might reject Jesus and Paul, but they had to submit to the authority of Scripture; therefore, Paul confronted them with the Word of the Lord. From Holy Writ he proved that Jesus was the Messiah. He reasoned with them out of the Scriptures, not out of the fancies of his head. What he had to say was logical and orderly, but it was not the product of human reason; it was the subject of divine revelation. Paul made use of his intellectual capacities in his presentation, but he did not allow his logical deductions to take him beyond the teaching of Scripture.

From the record in Acts we learn something about the content of Paul's preaching. He preached Christ, not social involvement. His principal subject was the suffering, death, resurrection, and messiahship of Christ (verse 3). Furthermore, the Christ whom he preached is the Christ of the Bible, not just the Christ of human experience. You would think that the Christ whom many people profess to know is the Christ of Scripture, but such is not necessarily the case. It is

11

possible to embrace a philosophical Christ by an irrational leap of faith. But that kind of Christ is just a projection of the human imagination. The Christ who saves sinners is the historical Christ whom God glorified and exalted to be a Saviour and a prince.

This is one of the perversions of neo-orthodoxy and the dialectical theologians.

A favorable response to the preaching of the gospel is never unanimous. When the truth as it is in Jesus reaches sinners' ears, "some" believe (verse 4). We cannot expect that everyone will receive the love of the truth, even though God has commanded all men to repent and believe. Many repudiate and reject it and continue in their obstinate rebellion against the truth. The great wonder is that any believe. How do you account for it? We have a clue in the Greek word *proskleroo,* translated "consorted" in verse 4. It means that some were assigned to Paul by divine decree—that is, their salvation was determined by God in His own eternal counsel.

Note the results of the sowing of the seed in Matthew 13:3-8. Only one-fourth produced.

Noteworthy is the fact that many Gentiles trusted Christ. Also of significance is the fact that Gentile women of social standing embraced the Saviour. Frequently women appear to be more easily persuaded of the truth than men are. It was true at Thessalonica and obvious yet today, for many churches would close their doors if it were not for the faithfulness of the women.

The reprobate Jews considered themselves too respectable to attack Paul openly, and so they incited the criminal element of the city to rioting (verse 5). City riots are an ancient and a modern scheme of the devil to bring disorder and chaos and make conditions impossible for the preaching of the gospel. In riots people throw off all natural restraints and give expression to their innate

Lawlessness and anarchy will characterize the last days of the

church on earth
and also the
tribulation
(II Timothy 3:3;
Matthew 24:12).

depravity. The mob at Thessalonica disregarded any semblance of legality by breaking into Jason's home, thinking to drag Paul into the street before the assembly. Not finding the preacher, they seized Jason (verse 6). Someone had to endure the brunt of their wrath, and they implicated Jason in the false charges.

How up-to-date the account reads. The riffraff succeeded in setting the city in an uproar and then lay the blame for it on the servants of God. They accused the evangelistic team of stirring up a social revolution. In one sense the missionaries had turned the world upside down, but not in the same sense that their opponents suggested. Their charges were plainly misrepresentations.

The Jews
accused Jesus of
the same thing
(John 19:12).

Evidently Paul had been instructing the believers in the doctrine of the Lord's return. He had been explaining to them that Christ would come as king to rule the nations. The hostile crowd construed these teachings to mean that Caesar had a competitor for the throne of Rome (verse 7). This gave rise to charges of sedition and insurrection. Inasmuch as Jason had aided and abetted a criminal, he too was liable to the wrath of Rome.

These reports reached the general public—the silent majority—and the civil magistrates, causing them to be alarmed and disturbed (verse 8). It is amazing how easily people are troubled by unsubstantiated rumors. People seem to have a predilection for being naturally suspicious of other people's motives and for believing anything they hear. They apparently want to believe the worst.

The Apostle Paul was not to be found. Evidence of Jason's complicity was not forthcoming. Consequently, someone paid Jason's bail, and he was released (verse 9). Paul took the uprising as a signal for departure from the city. Accompanied by Silas, he headed westward for Berea (verse 10). Timothy remained in Thessalonica to stabilize and strengthen the newly formed church. Thus began that ideal church to which Paul wrote two fascinating letters.

FOOD FOR THOUGHT

"Every heart with Christ is a missionary and every heart without Christ is a mission field."

—Dick Hillis

NOW TEST YOUR KNOWLEDGE

Matching:

1. _____ Paul's home

2. _____ Timothy's home

3. _____ Barnabas' native land

4. _____ Roman colony that was the seat of medicine

5. _____ Man in Paul's vision (Acts 16) was from here.

6. _____ City where Paul received orders to go to Europe

7. _____ Port city for Philippi

8. _____ Seized by mob in Thessalonica

9. _____ Accompanied Paul to Berea

10. _____ Remained in Thessalonica to establish and strengthen church

A. Philippi

B. Timothy

C. Macedonia

D. Cyprus

E. Tarsus

F. Silas

G. Jason

H. Troas

I. Lystra

J. Neapolis

CONGRATULATIONS TO AN IDEAL CHURCH

2

LESSON SCRIPTURE
I Thessalonians 1:1-10

RELATED SCRIPTURE
Ephesians 2:1-10; James 2:14-26

LESSON AIM
To demonstrate that genuine faith
produces godly followers.

LEARN BY HEART
"And ye became followers of us,
and of the Lord, having received the
word in much affliction, with joy of
the Holy Ghost"
(I Thessalonians 1:6).

EVERY DAY WITH THE WORD

Monday	Rest for labor	Matthew 11:25-30
Tuesday	Labor in the Lord	Romans 16:1-12
Wednesday	Laborers together	I Corinthians 3:1-10
Thursday	Abundant labors	I Corinthians 15:1-11
Friday	Fruit of labor	Philippians 1:19-30
Saturday	Fervent labor	Colossians 4:7-18
Sunday	Labor in the Word	I Timothy 5:17-25

STUDENT'S NOTEBOOK

This column is for
the student who
desires additional
study of the lesson
theme.

LESSON PREPARATION

In all probability the Apostle Paul wrote hundreds of letters during his lifetime, but only thirteen of them (fourteen if he wrote the book of Hebrews) bear the seal of divine authority and merit a place in the canon of Scripture. First Thessalonians falls in this category. Paul wrote it during his first visit to Corinth in about A.D. 50, approximately twenty years after his conversion, and sent the letter with Timothy to the believers at Thessalonica.

THE EPISTLE TO THE THESSALONIANS
(I Thessalonians 1:1-4)

Several distinctions characterize the first epistle to the Thessalonians. It is the only New Testament document which we are commanded to read (5:27). It is probably the first of Paul's inspired writings. The letter contains the earliest full discussion in Christian literature about the Lord's return. The subject of Christ's appearing occurs in every chapter, and each reference to it relates to a context of practical matters.

In chapter 1 the doctrine of the Lord's return produces examples (verses 7,10); in chapter 2 the doctrine promotes evangelism (verses 2,4,8,9,19); in chapter 3 this truth provides establishment (verses 2,13); in chapter 4 the prospect of His return provokes exhortation (verses 1,13-18); and in chapter 5 this doctrine prompts expectation (verses 4-6,23). All problems are to be solved and all conduct regulated in the light of the Lord's return.

The salutation of the letter contains the names of Paul, Silvanus, and Timothy (1:1a). "Paul" means "little." He may have been small of stature, but he was a spiritual giant. "Silvanus" (or Silas) means "of the forest" and speaks of abundance. "Timothy" (or Timotheus) means "God-fearing" and suggests that this young man had a significant designation to live up to.

Paul addresses this letter to "the church of the Thessalonians." The Greek word *ecclesia,* trans-

The book of Revelation promises a blessing to those who read it and keep it (Revelation 1:3).

Silvanus later became a secretary to the Apostle Peter (I Peter 5:12).

lated "church," refers to a called-out assembly of people. The word *ecclesia* is used in the New Testament in a nontechnical way of the Israelites in the wilderness and also of the mob at Ephesus. It more especially designates a local assembly of people who have been united to Jesus Christ and to each other by the baptizing work of the Holy Spirit. This is the significance here. Sometimes the word *ecclesia* is used in a regional sense, as "the churches of Galatia." On occasion the word takes on a much broader meaning and refers to all believers everywhere who belong to the body of Christ.

All Christians are, like the Thessalonians, related not only to God the creator but to God the Father (verse 1b). We have become the children of God by the new birth and the sons of God by adoption. We partake of our Father's nature and enjoy an intimacy with Him which permits us to call Him "Abba"—Father.

The fact that the preposition "in" before "God the Father" is not repeated in the Greek before "the Lord Jesus Christ" suggests the unique union which the Son of God has with the Father (verse 1c). It intimates His deity and equality with the Father. The fact that grace and peace come both from God and Jesus Christ supplies us with the strongest evidence that Jesus Christ is Himself God, for only God can dispense grace (verse 1d). Every time Paul thought of the Thessalonians, he breathed a prayer of gratitude to God for them (verse 2). God deserved to be thanked for whatever spiritual activities marked the Thessalonians, because God was working Christian graces and virtues in these young believers. They were responsible to be faithful, to labor, to love, to

Acts 7:38 uses the word *ecclesia*, but not in a theological or Pauline sense.

I Corinthians 16:1; II Corinthians 8:1

Ephesians 1:22; 3:10; 5:23-32; Acts 20:28

In John 1:12, note the word "become." We are not the children of God until we have been born of the Spirit.

Is this the way all of your former pastors felt about you?

hope, to persevere, to follow, to evangelize, and to wait for Christ. But for all of these accomplishments on their part Paul gave the credit to God because God was causing the Thessalonians to behave like this.

Especially did Paul remember their work of faith (verse 3a). Grammatically, this could mean "the work which is faith," for in a sense faith is a work (John 6:29). Likely, however, Paul meant that faith is the origin of good works. The Thessalonians were zealous of good works because they were genuine believers. Their works proved the reality of their faith. Their practice proved their profession. Their deeds were acceptable to God because they were accompanied by faith (Hebrews 11:6).

These same truths form the thesis of the book of James. Paul and James are in perfect harmony.

Paul also recalled their "labour of love" (I Thessalonians 1:3b). Work and labor are not synonymous. Work involves any task; labor stresses the exhaustion which getting the job done often demands. "Labor" implies the taxation of all our energies in the service of our Lord; it is mental, physical, and emotional strain. Love prompts this kind of toil. A believer's love for Christ can be measured by the amount of labor he is willing to contract.

Not only are we patient because of hope, but we also rejoice because of our hope (Romans 12:12). Hope keeps us happy.

Paul also reminisces about their "patience of hope" (verse 3c). They remained steadfast and steady under all sorts of pressure because of their hope in Christ. Hope, like faith, must have a proper object. It makes a great deal of difference whether you pin all of your hopes on human agencies, institutions, relationships, and promises or whether you place all of your hopes "in our Lord Jesus Christ." The expression "in the sight of God" indicates that their hope, faith, love, and patience were sincere—open to the scrutiny of the Father.

Perhaps this is the place to distinguish between faith and hope. Faith looks up; hope looks forward. Faith accepts; hope expects. Faith appropriates; hope anticipates. And this is as good a time as any to realize that when the Bible talks about faith, hope, joy, patience, love, and the other virtues, it is not referring to any qualities which were born in us. These are Christian graces which the Holy Spirit is producing supernaturally in God's born-again people.

Note the progression in this passage. Paul gives thanks—making mention (verse 2), remembering (verse 3),and knowing (verse 4). He can give thanks because he is certain that the Thessalonians are God's elect people. He knows that they are elect because their lives emphatically demonstrate it. Their election is grounded in the love of God. They are beloved of God.

The word "elect" means "to single out from among others."

THE EXAMPLE OF THE THESSALONIANS
(I Thessalonians 1:5-10)

The Thessalonians were model believers. They delighted the heart of Paul, who was responsible under God for the founding of the work at Thessalonica. All of his recollections of them were happy ones. They were examples in the way they received the gospel message (verses 5,6). Paul calls it "our gospel" because Silas, Timothy, and he were the messengers of good news about the significance of Jesus' death and resurrection. At other times Paul calls it "the gospel of God," "the gospel of Christ," "the gospel of salvation," "the gospel of the grace of God." Each qualifying

What are you contributing to make your church the ideal church?

The word "gospel" has a "go" in it.

Study Romans 10:14-17, and note I Corinthians 1:21.

I Thessalonians 2:13

I Peter 1:23

Use a concordance to find verses which speak of assurance, for instance Hebrews 6:11— "the full assurance of hope."

phrase emphasizes some particular aspect of the glad tidings.

It is important to realize that the gospel "came." The Thessalonians were once ignorant of the truth. The coming of the gospel was necessary for their salvation. No one can be saved apart from hearing and heeding the Word. It is also important to observe that when the gospel came, it came in words. No revelation from God can be definite without spoken or written words. But they were not mere words. They were not dead but dynamic words. They were not mere human words but words "which the Holy Ghost teacheth (I Corinthians 2:13). The Holy Spirit energized the Word so that it became effectual. The seed of the Word is the powerful instrument which the Spirit employs to regenerate those who are dead in trespasses and sins.

Paul preached the Word "in much assurance," and many of the residents of the city received the Word "in much assurance." The Holy Spirit was causing a resounding "Amen" to well up in the souls of the Thessalonians while they listened to the truths of the gospel. Apart from the illuminating and persuading work of the Spirit, no one would ever receive the Word—especially when receiving the Word would result in "affliction" (I Thessalonians 1:6) and contradict all the false notions which pagan philosophy taught.

The Thessalonians embraced the truth despite unfavorable circumstances. Although duress of persecution would naturally fill them with forebodings about their own safety and would, in the natural course of things, upset their emotional equilibrium, the Holy Spirit supernaturally filled them with a holy optimism and a radiant joy. Is it any wonder that these people became "followers" of the Lord?

Just as certainly as night follows day, so service follows salvation. When people receive Christ, they respond to His voice and follow Him. Sometimes they follow Him afar off, but they are still following Him. Genuine salvation results in a godly concern for others. The Thessalonians could not be content to enjoy the benefits of the gospel for themselves alone. As soon as they came to know Christ, they immediately undertook a program of home and foreign missions (verse 8). They sounded out the gospel in their own district in Macedonia. It spread to adjacent territory in Achaia, and then went to the regions beyond—"in every place."

It was never necessary for Paul to give the churches a report of what happened at Thessalonica when he first preached the gospel there. The believers around the Roman world could tell the story as well as Paul could, and they were, with Paul, convinced of the genuine conversion of these formerly pagan people, for they had "turned to God from idols" (verse 9). Notice the order. They did not turn from idols to God. In turning to Christ, they automatically turned their backs on everything that constituted their background, culture, and religion.

And how can we be so sure that they had really turned to God? Perhaps they were only pretending. Never! Their subsequent attitudes and activity proved their real conversion. They had formerly subjected themselves to the servitude of Christ. They owned and acknowledged a new master in the Lord Jesus Christ, and to Him they gave their heart's devotion (verse 9b).

The word "followers" here means "imitators."

John 10:3,4

The Thessalonians were like the sounding board in a piano. The notes of the gospel struck them and reverberated out to every place.

Think of some of the "gods" people are bowing down to today. Do you have any idols in your life?

Christ became the reason for their living and their hope when dying. Their conduct was regulated by the daily prospect that Christ would come to rescue them from the day of wrath (verse 10). Their past was dark and their present dangerous, but their prospect was glorious. Now they eagerly awaited the arrival of the same Jesus whom God had raised from the dead.

FOOD FOR THOUGHT

"Of all commentaries upon the Scriptures, good examples are the best and liveliest."
—John Donne

NOW TEST YOUR KNOWLEDGE

Find the triads:

1. The letter to the Thessalonians bore the names of: _____, _____, and _____.

2. Paul thanked God for the Thessalonians' work of _____, labor of _____, and patience of _____.

3. The gospel came to the Thessalonians in _____, in the _____, and in _____.

4. The news about the Thessalonians reached to _____, _____, and _____.

5. The conversion of the Thessalonians led them to _____, to _____, and to _____.

6. Jesus Christ will come from _____; He was raised from _____; and He will deliver us from _____.

IN DEFENSE OF EVANGELISM

3

LESSON SCRIPTURE
I Thessalonians 2:1-12

RELATED SCRIPTURE
II Corinthians 2:14—6:10

LESSON AIM
To do at least one thing to encourage a new convert in his walk with Christ.

LEARN BY HEART
"But as we were allowed of God to be put in trust with the gospel, even so we speak; not as pleasing men, but God, which trieth our hearts"
(I Thessalonians 2:4).

EVERY DAY WITH THE WORD

Monday	Believe the gospel	Mark 1:1-15
Tuesday	Publish the gospel	Mark 13:1-13
Wednesday	Obey the gospel	Romans 10:13-21
Thursday	Preach the gospel	I Corinthians 9:7-18
Friday	Live the gospel	II Corinthians 5:14-21
Saturday	Support the gospel	II Corinthians 9:1-15
Sunday	Defend the gospel	Philippians 1:3-17

STUDENT'S NOTEBOOK

This column is for the student who desires additional study of the lesson theme.

LESSON PREPARATION

At one time in his ministry Dr. G. Campbell Morgan confessed that he feared to talk to people who occupied high positions in society and culture. "Then," he said, "one night I knelt beside an old man whom sin had all but wrecked. I spoke to him of the cleansing blood of Christ, and of the possibility of his becoming a new creature in Christ. Presently someone said, 'Please, sir, speak to the other man kneeling beside you.' I turned and recognized the mayor of the city, who six weeks before had sentenced the oldster to a month's hard labor. Both men were equally lost. Both accepted Christ. The mayor joyfully shook hands with the old man and said, 'Well, we didn't meet here the last time!'

"The old man recognized the mayor and said, 'No, and we will never meet again as we did the last time! I'm a new man in Christ, and we are brothers.'

"That scene," said Dr. Morgan, "lingers with me yet. It removed my fear to speak to anyone about Christ."

THE MOTIVE FOR EVANGELISM
(I Thessalonians 2:1-6)

The Apostle Paul's two-week campaign at Thessalonica contains all of the earmarks of a Biblical and effectual evangelism—especially among some of the elite of that city. Verse 1 records the success of that initial effort among a pagan people—"it was not in vain." Literally the expression reads, "It has not come to be empty." The real test of the success of any gospel effort comes after the meetings are over and the decisions are weighed in terms of transformed lives. It is not the initial response that counts so much as the ultimate results. Are the decisions lasting? Do they issue in lives that bear fruit? If they do, then the endeavor may be called a success. Fireworks evangelism is like a rocket: it goes up in fire and

"The fear of man bringeth a snare: but whoso putteth his trust in the Lord shall be safe" (Proverbs 29:25).

The nobility responded (Acts 17:4). Note also I Corinthians 1:26.

Note that the decision of the Philippian jailer bore spiritual fruit as evidence of a real conversion (Acts 16:30-34).

falls like a dead stick. Holy Spirit led evangelism causes the dry and dead sticks to come alive and bear fruit.

Biblical evangelism inevitably leads to persecution (verse 2). When an evangelist enjoys universal acclaim, you have reason to wonder whether he is practicing the methodology of the Bible and preaching the whole truth of God's Word. The gospel has always been and always will be an offense to the natural man, and those who declare the whole counsel of God will never win many friends and influence scores of people in high places.

The doctrines of total depravity and sovereign grace are unacceptable and even abhorrent to the multitudes, and the evangelist who stresses these truths will find himself at odds with carnal people. In nearly every place where Paul preached he concluded his campaign by being driven from town. His kind of evangelism was not a status symbol or a sign of respectability. He was defamed, made as the filth of the world, and considered the offscouring of all things from the start to the finish of his stormy career (I Corinthians 4:13).

Find in the book of Acts the number of times Paul was compelled to make a quick exodus from town.

Neither physical abuse nor emotional stress can dissuade those whom God has called to the work of the gospel. Threats on their lives cannot silence them. The severer the opposition, the stronger they become in their denunciations of sin. Their courage is not a rash recklessness or brazenness; it is born of the Holy Spirit. God in grace supernaturally works a holy boldness in those whom he appoints to this ministry. They feel perfectly at home enunciating the great truths of redemption, and they confidently commend Christ to all who need Him.

They take Paul's attitude: "Woe is unto me, if I preach not the gospel!" (I Corinthians 9:16).

Romans is pre-eminently the gospel of God (Romans 1:1; 15:16).

The Biblical evangelist concerns himself with the "gospel of God." This expression suggests the source of the message: it originates from God and comes with the authority of God. It also implies the content of the message: it is a word about God's holiness, His wrath, His love, His grace, and His salvation. The messengers of it have no warrant from God to fill up the content of their message with stories, jokes, and small talk. They deal with theology—the doctrine of God—and press the claims of God upon sinners. They realize that they are engaged in a contest against the world, the flesh, and the devil. They are in the thick of the battle, not in practice maneuvers.

The announcer of the good news must not stray from sound doctrine (I Thessalonians 2:3). He must be well along the way to mastering the Word of God. Even if he leads people astray ignorantly, he will be held accountable for it. Woe to the man who gives sinners a false impression of the truth or wrests the Scriptures.

In verse 3, the word "deceit" suggests a wandering astray from sound teachings.

But an intelligent grasp of the truth is not enough. He must also live in harmony with the truth. He dares not deviate from moral purity. God requires that a useful vessel be a clean vessel. Those who speak the name of Christ must make a clean break with the filthiness of the flesh and spirit. An evangelist who tells dirty stories to his personal cronies is not a success even though he may move thousands to make decisions for Christ every year.

The soul winner likewise must stifle the temptation to get results by hook or by crook. He had better be careful what lures he uses to catch fish in the gospel net. Every trade has its own tricks, and modern evangelism is often guilty of ensnaring

In verse 3, the word "guile" implies "trickery." It means "to catch people under false pretenses or of giving them the wrong slant on what their decisions involve. The Christian life is not an exciting, thrill-a-minute, romantic adventure; it is a life of personal loss and sacrifice, of mortifying the deeds of the flesh, and of dogged persistence in the things of Christ. No true Christian is "carried to the skies on flowery beds of ease." Let's not hold out false hopes to people in our zeal to chalk up another convert on our growing list.

with bait."

Can you think of some of the fleshly appeals people use to entice unbelievers to become Christians?

The Biblical evangelist is not an untried and inexperienced novice in the work of the Lord (verse 4). He is a man who has been tested in the crucible of suffering and come out approved of God. Men are not ready to go into evangelistic work without an accurate knowledge of God, His Word, and human nature. Would-be evangelists would be wise to serve a hitch in a local church where they can prove their qualifications in a teaching ministry. The evangelist field is no place for a starry-eyed beginner.

See what kind of men Barnabas and Timothy were (Acts 4:36,37; 11:22-30; 13:1; Philippians 2:19-22).

Every candidate for an evangelistic ministry ought to search his heart to determine his hidden motives. Has God given him the gift of evangelism and specially appointed him to this ministry by an unmistakable leading? Or has he chosen this path of service for himself and by himself? Does he want supremely to please God? Or does he want the plaudits of men? Does he use soul winning for an excuse to make a name for himself and for getting local, national, or international prestige (verse 5)? Does he seek status (verse 6)? Or does he really have a burden for the lost? Does he think it is the one spot in Christian service where he can get rich quick?

THE METHOD OF EVANGELISM
(I Thessalonians 2:7-12)

In the New Testament sense of the word, "evangelism" is more akin to modern pioneer missions than to modern evangelism. Paul was preeminently an evangelist, for he endeavored to preach Christ in places where He had never been named. Paul was called to lay the foundation; pastors later built the superstructure upon the foundation which he had laid. A study of Paul's methods will help to explain why his ministry as an evangelist was so fruitful. An imitation of his methods even in the twentieth century might accomplish what all of our sophisticated technology in the service of missions has not yet produced.

The bearer of God's gospel must approach his prospects gently—not overwhelm them with the profundities of theology (verse 7). They have to be handled like babies. They need to be spoon-fed at the first. Unless they feel confident in the Christian worker and enjoy a friendly rapport with him, they may parrot the right prayer and give the right answers just to get him off their backs. The soul winner cannot lord it over the convert or adopt a superior air. He must convey a genuine warmth to the unconverted. He must woo them before he can win them.

Unchurched people can sense whether they are really loved. Soul winners cannot expect permanent results until they feel the kind of love for the lost—at least in a measure—that led Christ to sacrifice Himself for the ungodly (verse 8). Paul considered the Thessalonians so dear that he took great delight in making any sacrifice—even the

Romans 15:20

Study how Jesus approached the woman at the well (John 4:6-29).

"He that winneth souls is wise" (Proverbs 11:30).

Some of Paul's converts felt the same way about him. At one time the Galatians would have plucked out their

29

supreme sacrifice—for them. This is the kind of Calvary love that moves men to Christ.

eyes for Paul (Galatians 4:15).

The Biblical evangelist is always willing to forfeit his rights. Every minister of the gospel has a right to expect financial support. They that preach the gospel live by means of the gospel. But some situations require that the man of God supply his own necessities by taking manual labor (verse 9). No servant of God should consider himself above stooping to menial tasks. He is no hireling—working only for a love offering. Souls are more important to him than silver.

The God-called evangelist is not content to restrict soul-winning activities to an hour and a half each night of the campaign. He is forever at it—night and day, in season and out of season, when it is convenient and when it isn't, when he is rested and when he is exhausted, when he feels like it and when he doesn't.

II Timothy 4:2

The true messenger of the gospel pays special attention to the way he behaves while he is in the company of God's people (verse 10). He walks circumspectly not only in the presence of those who are without but in the presence of those who have already trusted Christ. Babes in Christ can become disillusioned by the unsavory reputations of the very men who led them to Christ. Soul winners have a testimony to maintain lest they become stumbling blocks to the weak.

The servant of the Lord cannot always act like a baby, a mother, or a brother. Sometimes he must act like a father and use the heavy hand of discipline (verse 11). Fathers who love their children chastise them, and men in the capacity of spiritual leadership have to be willing to correct as well as cuddle spiritual infants. Fathers cannot

Why is it an error to speak about Christians now building God's kingdom in the world and about bringing in the kingdom and about the kingdom being in the hearts of those who subject themselves to Jesus' present kingship?

hold their children by the hand indefinitely. The babies must learn to walk by themselves and walk in such a manner so as not to disgrace the family name. The prospects of reigning with Christ in His coming kingdom and sharing with Him in His eternal glory should provide sufficient incentives for any child of God to walk with the Lord in the light of His Word.

FOOD FOR THOUGHT

"You can hardly have evangelism unless you have Christian scholarship; and the more Christian scholarship you have, so much the more evangelism."

—J. Gresham Machen

NOW TEST YOUR KNOWLEDGE

Complete the following:

1. The real test of the success of an evangelistic campaign is _____

2. The natural man abhors the doctrines of _____
   _____
   and _____

3. A holy boldness is produced in the messenger of the gospel by _____

4. The New Testament concept of evangelism relates more especially to _____

5. Soul winners must maintain a good testimony to Christians because _____

Answer true or false:

6. Universal acclaim indicates that an evangelist is preaching the whole truth. _____

7. Paul often fled from the scene of his labors. _____

8. The "gospel of God" explains the source and authority of the gospel. _____

9. We will not be held accountable for what we do in ignorance. _____

10. Orthodoxy is more important than morality. _____

THE ENERGETIC WORD

4

LESSON SCRIPTURE
I Thessalonians 2:13-20

RELATED SCRIPTURE
II John 1-13; III John 1-14

LESSON AIM
To defend the truth and pass it
along to others.

LEARN BY HEART
"And ye shall know the truth, and
the truth shall make you free"
(John 8:32).

EVERY DAY WITH THE WORD

STUDENT'S NOTEBOOK

This column is for the student who desires additional study of the lesson theme.

Monday	Law of truth	Malachi 2:1-9
Tuesday	Spirit of truth	John 16:7-15
Wednesday	Word of truth	II Corinthians 6:1-10
Thursday	Love of truth	II Thessalonians 2:1-12
Friday	Knowledge of truth	I Timothy 2:1-15
Saturday	Ground of truth	I Timothy 3:14—4:10
Sunday	Way of truth	II Peter 2:1-16

LESSON PREPARATION

In the centuries before the first coming of Christ philosophers devoted their natural genius, as they still do, to the pursuit of truth. Where is ultimate truth to be found? How can absolute truth be recognized? Is any truth final, authoritative, and unchanging? Pontius Pilate had evidently given

33

some thought to this subject, for he inquired of Jesus, "What is truth?" Little did he dream that the solution to all of the mysteries about truth stood before him in the person of Jesus Christ.

Jesus announced that He had come into the world to reveal *the* truth. Christ is the personification of all truth. All truth is deposited in Him and dispensed by Him. He brought eternal, unchanging truth down to men and communicated it to men. Apart from Him human sagacity stumbles blindly in the dark. Apart from the preaching and teaching of the truth as it is in Jesus, men cannot lay hold of spiritual realities.

Jesus said, "I am the way, the truth, and the life" (John 14:6).

In Him are hid all the treasures of wisdom and knowledge (Colossians 2:3).

THE TRUTH HERALDED
(I Thessalonians 2:13-16)

Jesus Christ Himself is the living and true Word. The written Word of God is likewise the Word of truth. It is the only authentic source of the real truth about God's person, purposes, and program. The salvation of sinners is entirely dependent upon whether they hear redemptive truths and how they respond to them. Not all hear the truth, and not all who hear it heed it.

Christ is called Faithful and True (Revelation 19:11).

In verse 13 two different Greek words are translated "received." The first indicates an outward hearing or a mental awareness. The second means a hearty approval and appropriation of the truth. Sometimes this difference is expressed by the rather ambiguous terms "head knowledge" and "heart knowledge." Head knowledge—if we want to use this term—takes account of the historical facts; heart knowledge relies on the facts for personal salvation.

When anyone receives the Word of truth, God

In what sense do we believe with our heart? Certainly this has nothing to do with the physical organ.

deserves the thanks for it because God is responsible for it (verse 13a). God sees to it that those whom He has purposed to save actually encounter the Word—either through hearing it or reading it. Then God opens up the spiritual eyes to understand it and the spiritual heart to receive it. He operates inwardly to create a spiritual willingness to obey it. When people receive Christ, they receive Him willingly and gladly, but they have God to thank for the willingness with which they receive Christ.

This process never occurs apart from faith. It takes place "in you that believe" (verse 13c). However, faith is not the cause of the results; we are not saved on account of or by reason of our faith. Neither is faith the ground of salvation. Faith itself cannot save; God Himself saves sinners. He does it on the ground of the atonement, and He does it through the medium of faith and by means of the effectual Word.

Faith is decidedly a condition which the sinner must meet in order to be saved. But if the sinner were left to himself, he never would believe, and so God enables the sinner to meet His demands by effectually working faith in the sinner, using as His powerful instrument the energizing Word (verse 13b). Faith comes from God through the Word of God. No sinner can meet the conditions of faith, repentance, and obedience on his own. He must have divine assistance; and when it comes, he gives God thanks for it.

This kind of reception of the truth, produced by this kind of supernatural energy, always produces a Christian who keeps on believing the promises of God when he doesn't have at hand a single tangible evidence that God will keep His Word. The ef-

Ephesians 1:13

Acts 16:14

Philippians 2:13

In verse 13, the word "believe" is a present progressive participle,

35

fectual working of the Word produces the Christian who clings to Christ and perseveres in the things of Christ even when his relatives, neighbors, and friends use all their persuasive powers to turn him from Christ (verse 14). When ridicule and ostracism do not have their desired effect, the ungodly may even resort to physical violence as they did at Thessalonica and in Judea. But believers grow spiritually stronger in opposition. If professed believers lose their faith, they demonstrate thereby that the effectual Word was never really operating in them at all.

meaning "those who keep on believing." We keep on believing not in order to be saved but because we are saved. A godly faith is an enduring faith.

Verse 15 and 16 show the results when God removes all restraints from sinners and allows them to pursue the bents of their perversity and depravity. The minds of unregenerate people are so hostile toward God that, given the chance, they would murder Deity. Calvary proves not only that they would but that they did. Neither will they tolerate those who speak for God. Besides being God-haters, they are haters of mankind. Latent in their depravity are all the sins recorded in Romans 1 and Titus 3:3. If God should for a moment lift the restraints imposed by His Spirit, these corruptions would break out instantly and develop with fearful acceleration.

I Corinthians 2:8

Romans 8:7

Neither faith nor salvation is possible apart from the Word of faith and the gospel of salvation. To reach the Gentiles, Paul had to give them the wonderful words of life. But the Jews proved their hateful attitudes by attempting to deny the Gentiles an opportunity to hear (I Thessalonians 2:16a). It was one more sin that filled up the cup of God's wrath against the nation (verse 16b). Certain judgment awaited Jewry not only because they refused the outward calls of the gospel them-

Fear of punishment, loss of reputation, etc. restrains many people from doing what they yearn to do.

selves but also because they put obstacles in the way of the Gentiles in order to prevent them from being saved.

Paul's reference here to "saved" needs a word of explanation. The term "salvation" sums up and describes the spiritual and eternal deliverances which result from the intervention of God on behalf of those who trust Him. The word itself suggests a deliverance, and salvation is a deliverance from the penalty which sin incurs and a deliverance from the dominion which sin exercises.

THE TRUTH HINDERED
(I Thessalonians 2:17-20)

Under ordinary circumstances Paul's hasty departure from Thessalonica after only a very brief stay would have proved detrimental to the new work. Had the church at Thessalonica been established on the character of a man and been sustained by the dynamic of his personality, it would have collapsed in a short time. Paul's presence and supervision were not necessary to the survival of this church because it had a supernatural beginning and enjoyed a supernatural maintenance. The only safe and secure foundation for any local church is Jesus Christ. Ministries which are built upon Him rather than upon human leadership and empowered by the Holy Spirit do not decline when the pastor leaves.

Nevertheless the separations of this life are hard to bear and often difficult to understand (verse 17). With Paul it was not a case of "out of sight, out of mind." For him it was a case of "absence makes the heart grow fonder."

Evidently Paul's critics had accused him of run-

Their faith did not stand in the wisdom of men, but in the power of God. They were demonstrations of the Spirit's power (I Corinthians 2:4,5).

I Corinthians 3:11

In verse 17, the words "being taken" come from a Greek word meaning "being orphaned."

ning off and leaving the Thessalonian believers. It seems, in addition, that they were spreading the rumor that Paul cared nothing for the church and that he had no intention of returning. Such a report might hinder the growth of the church, and so Paul endeavored to counteract it by explaining how greatly he yearned to see them and how often he had laid his plans to come, only to be thwarted by the activities of his adversary (verse 18).

By no stretch of the imagination had Paul abandoned the Thessalonians. They were the cause of his exuberance. He hoped to receive the soul-winner's crown as the result of their conversion to Christ (verse 19). He looked upon them as the children whom God had given to him. They would be the stars in his crown and the flowers in his glorious garland. In that glory land, they would comprise his halo of gladness (verse 20).

FOOD FOR THOUGHT

"God requires us to give credit to the truths which He reveals, not because we can prove them, but because He reveals them."
—Daniel Webster

Match by placing letters in the blanks:

1. ____ The personification of truth
2. ____ Seekers after truth
3. ____ The nature of God's truth
4. ____ Instrument for conveying truth
5. ____ The ground of salvation
6. ____ The condition for salvation
7. ____ The meaning of salvation
8. ____ The result of salvation
9. ____ An evidence of salvation
10. ____ A means of restraint
11. ____ The soul winner's award
12. ____ The Christian's adversary

A. Absolute and ultimate
B. Atonement
C. Crown of rejoicing
D. Deliverance
E. Faith
F. Jesus Christ
G. Perseverance
H. Philosophers
I. Release from sin's power
J. Satan
K. The Holy Spirit
L. The Word of God

STABILIZING THE SAINTS

5

LESSON SCRIPTURE
I Thessalonians 3:1-13

RELATED SCRIPTURE
II Corinthians 1:1-14; Philippians
4:10-19

LESSON AIM
To lead a consistently holy life.

LEARN BY HEART
"Therefore, my beloved brethren, be
ye stedfast, unmoveable, always
abounding in the work of the Lord,
forasmuch as ye know that your
labour is not in vain in the Lord"
(I Corinthians 15:58).

EVERY DAY WITH THE WORD

Monday	Beauty of holiness	Psalm 29:1-11
Tuesday	Way of holiness	Isaiah 35:1-10
Wednesday	Spirit of holiness	Romans 1:1-17
Thursday	Fruit unto holiness	Romans 6:14-23
Friday	Created in holiness	Ephesians 4:17-29
Saturday	Continuance in holiness	I Timothy 2:1-15
Sunday	Partakers of holiness	Hebrews 12:3-15

STUDENT'S NOTEBOOK

This column is for the student who desires additional study of the lesson theme.

LESSON PREPARATION

The gyroscope is an amazing mechanical device which seems to defy the force of gravity. Chiefly it is used in navigation instruments for ships and aircraft. The gyrostabilizer is an adaption of the gyroscope which helps to keep aircraft and ships

The power of indwelling sin (the Adamic nature) has been likened to the downward pull of at sea from rolling in bumpy air and in rough water. Mounted in the hull, it keeps the vessel level by resisting any tendency toward tilting.

The prospect of the Lord's return acts upon the Christian like a gyrostabilizer. The belief that Christ may return today to call the child of God to account has its effect in preventing him from turning off course or from losing his equilibrium in the troubled waters of life. No matter how fiercely the waves of affliction beat against him, the believer whose life is regulated by his hope in Christ will neither lean nor drift.

APPREHENSION OVER CHRISTIAN STABILITY (I Thessalonians 3:1-8)

The Thessalonian believers were beginning to feel the full force of Satanic opposition, and Paul was uncertain about how they were weathering the storm. He feared that they might wander off course or flounder on the shoals of human opinion. So insufferable was his agitation at having to live in this suspense that he sent Timothy to find out whether his converts were maintaining their balance (verses 1,2). Paul's mental and emotional state proves that the Christian life is not all tranquility and calm. He did not assume the pious attitude of those who shrug off every unhappy circumstance with a glib "Well, praise the Lord, anyhow." He was deeply distressed and expressed it.

Under these conditions Paul resolved to surrender the society of Timothy for the greater good of the Thessalonians. He was willing to accommodate himself to adverse situations without thought for himself. It was not easy for him to lose a valuable helper. He felt abandoned in a

gravity. The power of the Holy Spirit working in us, however, neutralizes the effects of indwelling sin and keeps the Christian from inclining toward his baser appetites.

Paul admitted that he experienced fightings from without and fears from within (II Corinthians 7:5).

pagan city inimical to the gospel he preached, but he would not consider his own interests first. He put the needs of others before his own and thus obeyed the injunction which calls for us to prefer one another.

Romans 12:10

The Thessalonians needed to be reminded that suffering is the appointed destiny of Christians (verse 3). Note, however, that Paul does not say that Christians are appointed to wrath. Wrath will characterize the entire period of *the* tribulation, and from that wrath God has promised to deliver the church. He has promised us no such escape from persecution. Jesus said that as long as we are in the world we shall experience tribulation, or general troubles. God has ordained it for the believer's own good. Because suffering is not a pleasant experience, many Christians endeavor to avert it by lapsing into worldliness, compliance, and even denials of Christ.

I Thessalonians 5:9

I Thessalonians 1:10

John 16:33

II Corinthians 4:17; I Peter 1:6,7

In this connection, we should consider that Paul is talking about afflictions which God sends our way. Some Christians have from time to time displayed a morbid interest in suffering and have inflicted themselves with all sorts of unnecessary privations and tortures. Others have brought troubles upon themselves by their impetuosity or negligence. These afflictions are self-imposed and merit nothing of God's favor. But the afflictions which God directs our way to try our mettle are the means He employs to wean us away from earth and cultivate in us a longing for the coming of Christ and the land of eternal delights.

Knowing the utter inability of even dedicated Christians to stand unless God is continually putting forth fresh energies to hold them up and knowing the determination of the wily tempter to

Only God is able to make a man stand (Romans 14:4). If God should withdraw

His sustaining power for even a second, we would fall into sin.

overthrow the faith of God's people, Paul realized that spiritual defection among the Thessalonians was not an impossibility (verse 5). Temptation is a universal experience. It confronts all men from without; it arises in all men from within. From without the world and the devil appeal to our fleshly inclinations within. Sometimes God Himself puts some outward allurement in the path of the believer to test his character.

Some Christians have taught that it is no sin to be tempted but only to yield to temptations. That doctrine needs qualification. If a believer feels no inclination for what the temptation offers, he has not sinned in the temptation. But if the outward appeal meets with the slightest inward hankering for it, then the believer has indeed sinned. The great difference between our temptations and those of Christ comes to light right here. In every outward solicitation of the devil the Lord Jesus Christ felt a holy revulsion and not an atom of attraction for it. He had no inner appetite or affinity for it; we have.

By His gracious intervention God had sustained the faith and love of the Thessalonians. Timothy brought back this welcome information to the anxious Paul (verse 6). The qualities of faith and love are intrinsically "your faith and love." They are ours, for they originate in us and we exercise and exhibit them. But the gracious ministry of the Holy Spirit working mightily in us causes them to spring up and flourish. Faith and love, in the Bible sense, are not merely human attributes, natural impulses, or innate inclinations. They are aspects of the fruit of the Spirit which appear exclusively in Christians. Paul introduces us here to the kind of faith that works through love; it manifests itself

Colossians 1:29

Galatians 5:22,23

Galatians 5:6;
I John 3:18

43

in loving-kindness. God does not love others through us; He enables us to really feel love for them by creating, cultivating, and controlling the affections in our own souls.

The knowledge of the Thessalonians' faithfulness lifted Paul out of the doldrums (verses 6,7). They firmly stood their ground, neither yielding to the assaults of the tempter nor to the fawning persuasiveness of their unsaved countrymen. Nothing had shaken them from Him who was their true foundation. They had proved themselves to be truly regenerate and at the same time gave evidence that Paul's work among them had been a supernatural movement of the Spirit. Their stability stabilized Paul. Their spiritual victories became a source of strength to him (verses 7,8). We never know how much our faithfulness to God contributes to the building up of another believer's life. For better or for worse, others are depending upon our firmness and steadfastness.

Long-range results are the real proof of any soul-winning or revival effort.

ANTICIPATIONS ABOUT CHRISTIAN STABILITY (I Thessalonians 3:9-13)

In typical Pauline fashion, the apostle gave God thanks for everything—for the faith, love, memories, ambitions, and steadiness of the Thessalonians; for, after all, by His grace God had made them what they were. They were His workmanship and not the product of their own doing. Paul felt that he could never return sufficient thanks to God for all that He had wrought in the lives of his converts (verse 9). Are we equally as thankful when God causes spiritual virtues to appear in the souls of our acquaintances? Do we commend Him or them?

Ephesians 2:10 is the great proof-text against the idea of a self-made Christian. We owe everything good in us to the grace of God.

The spiritual successes of the Thessalonians increased not only Paul's gratitude but also his gladness. Some Christian leaders would have been unhappy to find out that their followers could climb to spiritual heights without them. Isn't it characteristic of carnality that some leaders would rather that their followers falter and fail than succeed without their supervision and suggestions. Such people take pride not in what the converts are accomplishing under God but in what they themselves are contributing to the successes. This is a selfish satisfaction.

It flatters the ego of carnal leaders that their followers cannot get along without them.

The Thessalonians were a credit to the gospel, but they were not perfect (verse 10). They had not reached an impasse in their Christian lives in which no further development was possible. Neither their faith nor their love nor any other spiritual quality in them was beyond improvement or enlargement. Regeneration did not immediately overcome all their deficiencies. Regeneration does not infuse right thinking and feeling and acting. It does not destroy the carnal inclinations which we inherited from Adam. Fleshly elements still enter into everything we think and do and are. We still pray selfish prayers, rejoice in self-gratification, and love others out of selfish motives. We cannot have perfect faith, perfect love, perfect joy, perfect stability, or perfect obedience until God eradicates the Adamic proclivities in us. This awaits either death or the rapture.

Philippians 3:12

Romans 7:17,20,25

God demands this kind of perfection, but because we are incapable of rendering it, He has clothed us with the perfect righteousness of Christ. In Him we have a perfect standing and lack nothing.

Meanwhile we are progressing toward the goal of perfection as the Holy Spirit retrains our Adamic inclinations and causes us to increase and abound in love (verse 12). He is continually working upon our affections, generating more and more the kind of feelings which are in harmony with God's Word and will. He effects these gracious operations in conjunction with the written Word and the believer's yieldedness to His ministrations.

Whatever transformation the Holy Spirit produces in the soul, He does for the grand object of making us inwardly holy (verse 13). Without holiness no man can see the Lord; but sinners as vile as we cannot make ourselves holy, and so God has given us the Spirit of holiness who has undertaken to produce His own moral qualities in us—and He is pleased to do this gradually, not instantly.

At the time of our regeneration we were sanctified wholly and perfectly only in the sense that God gave us this exalted standing. But in a practical sense we are not yet perfectly holy, nor will we ever be in this mortal life. We are growing progressively holy as well as progressively patient, gentle, joyous, loving, calm, etc. The prospect of the Lord's return and our having to give an account of our attitudes and attributes to Him supplies us now with the incentive we need in order to apply all those means which contribute to our growth in holy demeanor even though the flesh nature still tenaciously clings to us.

Whether he would fulfill his dream of an early visit to the Thessalonians or not, Paul knew that the spiritual progress of the believers did not depend upon him. He longed to visit them to perfect their faith, but ultimately it was the Lord who would "make you to increase and abound in love." Paul did not say "to the end *I* may stablish your hearts" but "to the end *he* may stablish your hearts." The spiritual welfare of God's people is in the capable hands of God.

> Yieldedness is not the cause of these ministrations, but it is integral to them and a necessary condition.

FOOD FOR THOUGHT

"Our strength is shown in the things we stand for. Our weaknesses are shown in the things we fall for."

—Hugh A. Cowan

NOW TEST YOUR KNOWLEDGE

Answer in your own words:

1. Why was Paul so distressed at Athens? _____
   _____

2. Why did Paul send Timothy to Thessalonica? ____
   _____

3. Why does God send afflictions to believers? _____
   _____

4. What are the sources of temptation? _____
   _____

5. How does the Biblical concept of love differ from merely natural love? _____
   _____

6. Why did Paul thank God for the love, faith and steadfastness of the Thessalonians? _____
   _____

7. Why can't believers be completely obedient, completely faithful, completely patient, etc.? _____
   _____

8. What is the Holy Spirit's grand object in His gracious ministrations to the believer? _____
   _____

9. How does the prospect of the Lord's return relate to our growth in holiness? _____
   _____

10. Ultimately, who alone can establish the Christian?
    _____

A NEW PLEA FOR THE OLD MORALITY

LESSON SCRIPTURE
I Thessalonians 4:1-12

RELATED SCRIPTURE
I Corinthians 5:1-13; 6:9-20; 7:1-40

LESSON AIM
To relate the sanctifying ministry of the Holy Spirit to the believer's personal chastity and his love for others.

LEARN BY HEART
"For God hath not called us unto uncleanness, but unto holiness" (I Thessalonians 4:7).

EVERY DAY WITH THE WORD

Monday	Walk in fear	Acts 9:20-31
Tuesday	Walk in newness	Romans 6:1-10
Wednesday	Walk in the Spirit	Galatians 5:16-26
Thursday	Walk in love	Ephesians 5:1-18
Friday	Walk in wisdom	Colossians 4:1-6
Saturday	Walk in light	I John 1:1-7
Sunday	Walk in truth	III John 1-6

STUDENT'S NOTEBOOK

This column is for the student who desires additional study of the lesson theme.

LESSON PREPARATION

Modern society takes it pretty much for granted that contemporary circumstances should dictate moral behavior. "Situation ethics" is the term which describes the popular approach to questions of right and wrong. The advocates of this "new morality" never inquire whether conduct squares with an authoritative and abiding code of morality. According to them, this is old-fashioned and Victorian. They consider only whether the action is the result of a personal, responsible decision in a particular, present circumstance.

Our times parallel the morality of first-century society. Pagan people, although highly civilized, were preoccupied with sex. Sexual sins were as lightly condemned then as they are now. Sexual satisfaction outside the bonds of marriage was taken as a matter of course. Hardly a voice cried out in protest against homosexuality and other perversions. The Romans and the Greeks were so devoted to objects of art which were so obscene that modern archaeology is embarrassed to put them on public display.

The Thessalonian believers came from this kind of background. They had been regenerated, but this was only the initiation of the Christian life. They needed to conform more and more to the eternal standard of God's revealed will. Hence, the Apostle Paul proceeded to lay down divine restraints and regulations for their moral behavior. That same Word still determines moral values today and sits in judgment upon those who flout its authority.

A PLEA FOR CHASTITY
(I Thessalonians 4:1-8)

The Pauline epistles characteristically commence with details of doctrine and conclude with matters of deportment. First Thessalonians is no exception. In verse 1 the word "furthermore" [literally, "as for the rest"] marks a transition in

How much of your conduct, styles, habits, hobbies, philosophy, etc., is dictated by the mood of the age?

Hebrew society was a notable exception to the rule. In matters of morality Hebrews stood in sharp contrast to the pagans.

the letter. The main section (chapters 1—3) finishes, and the subsidiary section (chapters 4—5) begins. Paul's remarks to the Thessalonians took the form of a friendly entreaty; what he had to say pertained to their whole manner of life—their walk.

It is significant that the believer's conduct in the world is consistently described in the New Testament as a walk. This speaks of movement and progress. Standing still results in a tendency to backslide. The walk suggests an unspectacular advance; it involves no fanfare, nothing unusual, just a normal course. The walk does not specify any particular behavior; it entails everything a Christian does. Other passages of Scripture enjoin the child of God to walk in the light, walk circumspectly, walk in love, walk in the Spirit, walk in newness of life, walk in wisdom, and walk in truth.

The Galatians at first made such a spectacular advance that Paul speaks of them as running well. Sad to say, they soon got short of breath (Galatians 5:7).

The frequent exhortations of God's special servants are a necessary part of our learning to behave in a manner that will please Christ. The Thessalonians needed prodding and urging to assure their progress in the Christian faith. God intends that brothers in the Lord exhort one another to fresh efforts in the pursuit of godliness. But Christians who exhort others should remember that they have no authority of their own; they derive it from the Lord Jesus. They should also remember that they themselves are men of like passions, and so they need to exhort in a spirit of meekness, considering their own weaknesses.

Exhortation is a supernatural gift which certain Christians receive from the Spirit (Romans 12:8).

Galatians 6:1

In verse 2 observe that Paul did not say, "For ye know what commandments the Lord gave you by us." Paul gave the orders; of course, they

Paul delivered only what he had received from

Christ (I Corinthians 15:3).
Paul's orders are the equivalent of Christ's orders (I Corinthians 7:12).

originally came from Christ, who authorized Paul to transmit them. God expressed His will for the believer's walk in the form of commandments. The Christian must conform to divine law, and the supernatural operation of the Spirit of God in him enables him to obey God's law.

By "commandments," however, we are not to think of the Ten Commandments or any of the Mosaic legislation. Christ annulled the Mosaic law; it is now obsolete. But this does not mean that the saints of the church age are responsible to no code of conduct. They are in-lawed to Christ and obligated to adhere to the law of love. Genuine Christians keep the New Testament commandments and do not find them grievous; indeed, they love to do God's will. This relationship to the commandments is a proof of their regeneration.

Romans 10:4

Galatians 5:13,14

I John 5:3

I John 2:3

It is appropriate that Paul should introduce the subject of sanctification at this point, for without the work of sanctification none of the regenerate could obey the commandments (verse 3). The Holy Spirit's object in sanctifying God's elect is to bring them "unto obedience" (I Peter 1:2). "We keep his commandments, and do those things that are pleasing in his sight" (I John 3:22) because the sanctifying influences of the Spirit are causing this response in us. It is God's will for believers to love Him supremely and their neighbors as themselves. Only the sanctifying ministry of the Spirit can bring this about in us.

Christ does not do the obeying for us. We do the obeying, but the Holy Spirit puts a love in our hearts for the commandments and then inclines our wills to obey them.

God wills that Christians abstain from moral impurities of every sort—fornication in particular. By His sanctifying power the Holy Spirit implants a holy abhorrence for sin in the believer's soul. The Spirit delivers him from the love of sin as well as from its dominion. Purity is possible only to the

Remember, however, that indwelling sin inclines us in the

extent that the Holy Spirit works the principle of holiness in us and to the extent that the child of God submits to His cleansing and renewing operations.

The Christian's ability to "possess his vessel" depends upon the work of sanctification (I Thessalonians 4:4). God demands that we honor Him in our bodies, which belong to Him by creation and redemption. Without the sanctifying influences of the Spirit we could neither present our bodies to God nor honor Him with them. The church is espoused to Christ as a chaste virgin, and the Holy Spirit has pledged Himself to maintain that chastity.

Man's sexual appetites were damaged and distorted by the Fall. As a result he gives himself over to lust in utter abandonment, prostituting his God-given capacities to base ends for self-gratification (verse 5). Regeneration itself does not remedy this situation. Man needs supernatural power to maintain restraints upon his bodily passions so that he does not indulge them as the heathen do. The sanctifying ministry of the Spirit works to this end.

The person who commits an immoral act "defrauds" his brother (verse 6). He has cheated another of his rights and robbed him of his honor. Sexual familiarity outside the bonds of marriage is an injustice which God will repay with retribution. Those who refuse to live within the boundaries of moral law will have to pay the dire consequences of their wickedness. The Holy Spirit is cultivating in Christians the principle of love for others. Illicit relationships violate the law of love and deprecate Him who produces it.

God's purpose in saving us from sin's penalty is

opposite direction. The power of indwelling sin and the person of the Holy Spirit are always at war in the Christian (Galatians 5:17).

Acts 15:29;

II Corinthians
12:21; Ephesians
5:3,5; Colossians
3:5

to save us also from its pollution He has called us to be holy (verse 7). He planned that we should live in a holy atmosphere. Sanctification is the very air we breathe. Holiness is much more than a legal standing which we enjoy in Christ. It is also something experiential which occurs in us and changes us. Believers are holy in Christ, and they are also holy in themselves by virtue of the Spirit's working His own holiness in their dispositions, desires, and demeanor. Sanctification from start to finish is all the work of God—a work of sovereign grace and supernatural power. Woe be to the person who belittles this mighty work, for he has insulted the Spirit of holiness whom God has given to conform us to His own holy character (verse 8).

A PLEA FOR CHARITY
(I Thessalonians 4:9-12)

Sanctification is God's means of preserving the believer's chastity and also of cultivating a charitable disposition toward the Christian brotherhood (verse 9). By His power the Spirit of God enables us to feel for others a self-denying, self-giving love *(agape);* we love in the Spirit. He also works in our affections to produce a philanthropic love *(philadelphia)*—a love distinguished by acts of liberality and benevolence toward the poor and the afflicted. Such a love manifests itself in deeds, mutual concern and respect, hospitality, sympathy, and generosity. This kind of behavior is "God-taught"—that is, it is the result of the Spirit's work in the heart rather than the result of formal instruction.

God-taught love reaches out in ever-widening circles. It extends first to "one another" and then

God has given to
us the Spirit of
love (II Timothy
1:7).

Christ has taught
us what kind of
love this is by
His own example
(Ephesians 4:21;
5:2).

to "all the brethren." It embraces the local church and also the mission field—"in all Macedonia." There is no limit to its capacity, for it increases "more and more" (verse 10). Growth in love suggests the progressive side of sanctification, which is a gradual development in the virtues and graces of the Spirit. Little by little the Holy Spirit purges our affectionate nature of selfishness so that our love becomes ever purer and progresses toward perfection. In this life, of course, no Christian, however spiritual, loves either God or others perfectly; but as the Holy Spirit infuses divine love in his soul, the Christian feels an increasing love for God, for fellow believers, and for the unregenerate. Furthermore, he exercises that love by appropriate behavior toward them.

Paul prayed that believers might be "rooted and grounded in love" (Ephesians 3:17). See also Philippians 1:9, where love is intelligent and discreet. Love must be directed and controlled by knowledge, and knowledge comes by saturating ourselves with the Word of God.

Tranquility is an exhibition of this quality of love. Love prompts the Christian to strive strenuously to be still (verse 11). Quietness is the opposite of an excitable disposition and a feverish anxiety which disturbs the peace of others. Industry is also a distinguishing feature of love. It makes the believer so conscious of his own duties that he has no time to meddle in the affairs of others. Love will not permit us to neglect the daily round and routine of manual labor. It urges us to occupy until Jesus comes.

Decency is another earmark of love. It inspires the Christian to be circumspect in his behavior for the sake of unregenerate spectators. What will the unsaved neighbor think if believers give the impression of being restless, lazy, meddlesome, and financially dependent upon others? Believers are responsible to work for what they get. They dare not sponge upon more affluent Christians, for this is clearly an abuse of love. Love will not take advantage of the kindnesses of others. Indolence endangers the relationship of love. Let's not appear to be beggars and idlers, expecting someone else to provide for our needs or give us special discounts. The rule of thumb for Christians is that they "abstain from all appearance of evil."

The Thessalonians believed that the return of Christ was imminent, and they allowed the anticipation of this spectacular event to detract them from practical duties. In view of the approaching day of glory, hard work seemed to many of them to be inglorious and commonplace. But they, like us, needed to be reminded of the dignity of honest labor. Their diligence would impress unsaved neighbors, it would give them less time to interfere in the business of other people, and it would afford them the necessities of life. The prospect of the Lord's return was never intended to give Christians an excuse to while away the time. Rather, such a prospect is a boon to industry, integrity, and a healthy independency.

FOOD FOR THOUGHT

"Love is a wonder-worker, but it gets along better when it has brains to direct it."
—Billy Sunday

NOW TEST YOUR KNOWLEDGE

Give short answers:

1. What is the new morality called? _____
2. What word refers to the initiation of the Christian life? _____
3. What word describes the totality of a believer's demeanor in the world? _____
4. In what form does God express His will for the believer? _____
5. What work of the Spirit brings believers to obedience? _____
6. What word denotes sexual intimacies between unmarried people? _____
7. What law does sexual immorality violate? _____ _____
8. In what practical ways does love exhibit itself? __ _____

FAMILY REUNION IN THE SKIES

7

LESSON SCRIPTURE
I Thessalonians 4:13-18

RELATED SCRIPTURE
John 14:1-3; II Corinthians 5:1-10;
I John 3:1-3

LESSON AIM
To distinguish between the rapture
of the church and the second coming; to delineate the details of the
rapture.

LEARN BY HEART
"When Christ, who is our life, shall
appear, then shall ye also appear
with him in glory" (Colossians 3:4).

EVERY DAY WITH THE WORD

STUDENT'S NOTEBOOK

This column is for
the student who
desires additional
study of the lesson
theme.

Monday	Hope of the promise	Acts 26:1-8
Tuesday	Hope of Israel	Acts 28:17-24
Wednesday	Hope of glory	Romans 5:1-11
Thursday	Hope of righteousness	Galatians 5:2-15
Friday	Hope of the gospel	Colossians 1:15-23
Saturday	Hope of salvation	I Thessalonians 5:8-24
Sunday	Hope of eternal life	Titus 3:1-7

LESSON PREPARATION

Few places are as dreary as a graveyard. It is
often the scene of sadness and hopelessness,
especially if the interment involves an unsaved
person. The funerals of the heathen are charac-
terized either by a stoic indifference or the wail of

inordinate grief; for although pagan people entertain some ideas about the perpetuation of life beyond the grave, they enjoy no ringing certainty such as Christians possess. The gospel first brought immortality to light. The resurrection of Christ is the believer's guarantee that he, too, will experience a dramatic victory over death.

II Timothy 1:10

The resurrection of the saints was not a new doctrine (Acts 23:6; 24:15; 24:21; 26:6-8).

The Thessalonians had no doubts about the resurrection of the believers in their number who had died. But they were greatly troubled about the relationship of the deceased to the Lord's return. Would their departed loved ones forfeit participation in the return of Christ and the millennial kingdom? To this problem Paul next addressed himself.

THE BLESSED HOPE
(I Thessalonians 4:13-15)

During the interval of the Lord's absence Christians can expect that from time to time they will suffer bereavements. But they are not to think of the home-going of the saints as death. Rather, the deceased have fallen asleep in Jesus. "Sleep" is more than a euphemism for death. It suggests that death for the child of God is no longer a terror. Christ tasted death in all of its harsh horror in order to remove the sting of death for those who trust Him. Through what Jesus has done the substance of death has been reduced to a shadow.

Nevertheless, death is still an enemy (I Corinthians 15:26).

The death of a loved one in Christ must never be the occasion for gloomy despair. No cause exists for excessive and uncontrolled grief. Naturally, Christians feel real sadness at the loss of a dear one. Sighing and tears are normal and healthy. But continued and unchecked desolation con-

Even Jesus wept at the grave of Lazarus (John 11:35).

tradict the assurances and comfort which our hope in Christ affords.

Those who die before the Lord returns will not forfeit participation in His glorious appearing or in His kingdom reign. These disembodied spirits will accompany Christ at His return in the air. We have as much reason to believe this as we have to believe that Jesus died and rose again. Both are incontrovertible facts. Inasmuch as the disembodied saints come with Jesus, we must conclude that they have been with Jesus during the interval between their physical death and their bodily resurrection. They have been conscious in His presence and experiencing a "far better" state than what they enjoyed when they were physically alive.

The Christians who survive until Jesus comes have no advantage over those who have passed through the valley of the shadow of death. Living Christians will not precede the deceased Christians. God will compensate those who have had to face the dark valley by giving them a certain priority in the order of events. He will reunite their souls with their raised and glorified bodies before He translates the living to glory. In this blessed hope the living can rest.

The use of the pronoun "we" throughout this passage gives us occasion to wonder whether the Apostle Paul expected to be alive at the time of the Lord's return. Twice he classified himself with those "which are alive and remain." Some Bible teachers take the view that Paul did not intend to include himself at all, and that he simply referred to those of a distant generation who would be alive. This view holds that Paul eventually gave up any hope of being alive at the time of the Lord's return.

Philippians 1:23

In Psalm 23:4 the valley is a tunnel, not a terminal. "Though I walk" leaves it uncertain that all will die. Some will be glorified without dying, and David leaves room for it.

59

It seems much closer to the truth, however, that Paul entertained a reasonable expectation of being alive for this occasion, but he had never received positive assurance from the Lord that he would survive. He assumed the attitude of Christians in every generation that Christ would come in his lifetime. He hoped to be glorified without undergoing the nakedness of the disembodied state. He was absolutely certain that if he died he would be raised; but he was not so certain that he would "attain unto the resurrection" (literally, "arrive at the outresurrection")—that is, be alive at the time of the rapture.

Twice in II Corinthians 5 Paul expressly stated that he was looking forward to being "clothed upon" with his glorified body without dying (verses 2,4). Consider also Philippians 3:11.

THE GLORIOUS APPEARING
(I Thessalonians 4:16-18)

It is important that we distinguish between the second coming and the rapture. These are two separate and distinct events. Some Bible teachers prefer to think of the rapture of the church as a phase of the second coming. They speak of the second coming as occurring in two stages. Others make a special point of detaching it altogether from the second coming in order to avoid confusion. At any rate, the two events are quite distinguishable.

The second coming is a subject of Old Testament revelation; the rapture is not. The second coming is an occasion for mourning; the rapture is an occasion of joy. The second coming occurs at the end of the tribulation (a posttribulational coming); the rapture occurs before the tribulation (a pretribulational coming). The second coming brings Christ to the earth; the rapture brings Him to the air. The second coming regathers Israel from the four directions of the compass to a cen-

Zechariah 14:4

Matthew 24:31

Revelation
6:16,17

Matthew 24:3

I Thessalonians
3:13

Matthew
13:41-43;
24:39-41; 25:30,46

In a sense,
rapture is a good
word, because
the church will
be carried away
bodily.

Conceivably,
Satan might
marshall his
demon hosts in
an effort to
oppose the

tral location in Palestine; the rapture gathers the saints up into the air. The second coming entails the wrath of the Lamb; the rapture affords escape from the wrath to come. The second coming will be preceded by specific signs which will indicate its nearness; no signs will precede the rapture.

At the rapture Christ will come *for* His saints; at the second coming Christ will come *with* the saints whom He has previously raptured. The rapture pertains exclusively to the church; the second coming involves saved and unsaved Jews and Gentiles, Satan, and angels. At the rapture the saved will be removed from the earth and the wicked will remain on earth; at the second coming the wicked will be removed and the saved will remain.

In verses 16 and 17 Paul most emphatically is not talking about the second coming; he is discussing the rapture of the church. The word "rapture" is a bit deceiving. Nowadays it suggests a rhapsody or an ecstasy, being carried away emotionally; and so, perhaps it is not the best rendition of the Greek word translated "caught up." The Greek word is *harpadzein,* meaning "to seize" or "to snatch" as a thief would do in a robbery. In fact, the translators render a form of this Greek word "robbery" in Philippians 2:6. The rapture of the church will constitute the greatest "robbery" this world has ever seen, for Christ is coming to snatch away the pearl of great price which He purchased with His precious blood.

The Latin equivalent of *harpadzein* is *rapere.* The English word "rapture" comes from *rapere* and originally meant "the act of conveying a person from one place to another" *(Oxford Dictionary).* It will occur without warning, so suddenly that Satan will not be able to oppose it and so suddenly that Christians will have no time to make last-minute preparations to meet the Lord.

The rapture, then, will proceed as follows. The Lord personally will descend to effect the removal of the church; angels will not execute this miracle. A shout will be the first indication that the rapture is about to occur. No other signs will precede it, and for this reason many call the event "the secret rapture." But this does not mean a noiseless event. Others use the term "secret rapture" to signify the fact that the truth of it was a mystery (secret) hidden in the heart of the Trinity and revealed only in apostolic times. The shout is a cry of triumph and joy, for a great reunion with Christ and loved ones ensues. Perhaps some Christians will do some shouting about spiritual realities for the first time.

In all likelihood, however, Christ will give the shout in order to awaken the Christian dead from their graves and to attract the attention of the living saints. It will require a shout to wake drowsy Christians up. Paul says it is already "high time to awake out of sleep: for now is our salvation nearer than when we believed" (Romans 13:11). But, sad to say, some Christians will snooze on until they are aroused by the call of Christ at His coming, and they will be greatly embarrassed by their inattentiveness and carelessness.

An archangelic voice will also sound. Michael is the only archangel which Scripture names, and so we conclude that he will be present. He figures prominently as the leader of the invisible hosts of righteousness against the rulers of darkness. His presence at the rapture may be needed to thwart any attempt of the devil to hinder the resurrection of the dead and the rapture of the living. A blast

rapture, if he knew when it would occur. Colossians 2:15 seems to indicate that the demon forces tried to hinder Christ from passing through the airways to the Father's house.

I John 2:28; 4:17

Only Michael and Gabriel are named in Scripture.

upon the trump of God will provide the signal for the church to begin its ascent through space.

The participants in this resurrection and rapture are exclusively those who are "in Christ"—that is, church saints. The bodies of Old Testament saints will remain in their graves until the second coming of Christ (at the end of the tribulation period). Just as the Head of the body (Christ) was raised out from among other dead saints, so the members of the body (the church) will be raised out from among other dead saints (the Old Testament dead) who will not arise at this time. All the righteous dead will participate in the first resurrection, but the first resurrection will occur in three stages: Christ the firstfruits, those who are "in Christ" (church saints), and those who are Christ's (Old Testament saints and tribulation martyrs).

The living and the dead church saints will meet together in the skies in glorified bodies—bodies like unto Christ's glorious body. All will be changed, for corruption (the dead) will put on incorruption and mortality (the dying) will put on immortality in a moment, in the twinkling of an eye. Instantly, the bodies of both the dead and the living will be fitted for the conditions of the eternal state. The body is such an indispensable part of our being that even in Heaven we cannot be complete without it.

In the instant of glorification, the living will experience an eradication of the Adamic sin nature. They will enter upon the final phase of their sanctification in which every sinful blemish will be removed and they will enjoy perfect holiness. In the earthly life, the soul dominates, and the body is suited to it; in the Heavenly life, the spirit will

How appropriate that the members of the body should have the same kind of resurrection as the Head of the body!

Philippians 3:21; I John 3:2

I Corinthians 15:51,52

dominate, and the body will be suited for it—hence, our bodies will be "spiritual" bodies. They will not be vapors, mists, or ghosts. They will be material, physical, tangible bodies, but dominated by the principle of spirit and no longer subject to the ravages of time, restricted by the barriers of space, or restrained by material obstacles.

FOOD FOR THOUGHT

"There is no medicine like hope, no incentive so great, and no tonic so powerful as expectation of something better tomorrow."
—O. S. Marden

NOW TEST YOUR KNOWLEDGE

Give short answers

1. What is the condition of the dead now?_____
    _____

2. What brought immortality to light? _____
    _____

3. How do Christians think of death? _____
    _____

4. What do we call the resurrection of all the righteous? _____

5. At what event will Christ return to the earth with His saints?_____

6. At what event will Christ return in the air for His saints? _____

7. At the rapture who will be removed and who will be left behind? _____
    _____

8. At the second coming who will be removed and who will be left behind? _____
    _____

9. What does the Greek word *harpadzein* mean? ____
    _____

10. What do we mean by the "secret" rapture? _____
    _____

MOMENTOUS DAYS AHEAD

8

LESSON SCRIPTURE
I Thessalonians 5:1-11

RELATED SCRIPTURE
II Corinthians 4:1-18; I John 1:5-7

LESSON AIM
To show what relationship the rapture sustains to the tribulation period; to fortify the believer's hope in full salvation.

LEARN BY HEART
"For God hath not appointed us to wrath, but to obtain salvation by our Lord Jesus Christ"
(I Thessalonians 5:9).

EVERY DAY WITH THE WORD

Monday	Day of fierce anger	Isaiah 13:1-16
Tuesday	Day of vengeance	Isaiah 63:1-6
Wednesday	Day of calamity	Jeremiah 46:20-28
Thursday	Day of trouble	Ezekiel 7:1-12
Friday	Day of the Lord	Amos 5:12-20
Saturday	Day of alarm	Zephaniah 1:7-18
Sunday	Day of wrath	Romans 2:1-11

STUDENT'S NOTEBOOK

This column is for the student who desires additional study of the lesson theme.

LESSON PREPARATION

Special days hold special significance for us all. We celebrate the anniversaries of our birthday and wedding day. We remember our departed loved ones especially on Memorial Day. We welcome national holidays—Labor Day, Armistice Day,

The day that is most important to the Christian is the day when he passed from death to life. Do you have a date for your spiritual birthday?

Thanksgiving Day. We observe Mother's Day and Father's Day; the list seems endless. On the religious calendar hardly a day of the year is without some meaning—Reformation Day, All-Saints Day, Easter Day, Christmas Day.

Likewise, the Word of God attaches much importance to special days—man's day, the day of the Lord, the day of Christ, the day of salvation, the day of vengeance, and many more. The Scriptures give more space to descriptions of the day of the Lord than to any other day. It will be a unique period in world history, and Paul wanted the Thessalonian believers to understand the church's relationship to "that day."

THE DAY OF DESTRUCTION
(I Thessalonians 5:1-3)

Not even the angels know the exact time of the Lord's return (Matthew 24:36).

No one knows how long an interval will elapse before God will visit our planet with His fierce indignation. From the human perspective the "times and the seasons" are indeterminate (verse 1). We know as much about the time element as it is possible for us to know apart from a special divine revelation. God has been pleased to hide this information from us in order that we shall always live in a state of expectancy and preparedness.

Throughout the church age the Lord's people have always had reason to believe that the period of waiting would be short and that the Lord would return in their lifetime. Some religious enthusiasts, with more zeal than knowledge, have gone so far as to set exact dates for the return of Christ, but each has proved to be the victim of his own folly. We cannot know the day or the hour—no, not even the month or year or decade. It is the suspense of not knowing that keeps the Christian "on his toes"—always ready if the event should occur today.

The Old Testament gives much space to descriptions of the day of the Lord. Joel first used the term in connection with a destruction from the Almighty (1:15). The prophet revealed that a divine intervention would result in cataclysmic judgments which would involve the heavens and the earth (3:16). Later, Isaiah warned that before universal peace settled upon this planet, God would visit earth by acts of vengeance. Jeremiah called this period "the time of Jacob's trouble" (30:7). Daniel referred to it as "a time of trouble, such as never was since there was a nation" (12:1).

See the summaries in the NSRB concerning the day of the Lord, pages 929 and 1372.

Isaiah 2:10-19; 34:1-8; 63:1-6

Jesus described the day of the Lord as "great tribulation, such as was not since the beginning of the world to this time, no, nor ever shall be" (Matthew 24:21). The Scripture consistently testifies to the fact that this period will be introduced "as a thief in the night" (II Peter 3:10). It will come when the people of the world least expect it. It will come so suddenly that no one will have time to make last-minute preparations (I Thessalonians 5:2). Like the people of Noah's day, the inhabitants of earth will not be aware of their danger until they find themselves floundering in the judgment.

The tribulation is a period unprecedented, unparalleled, and unequaled in human history.

Matthew 24:37-39

Prospects for a universal peace will seem bright just before the day of judgment dawns (verse 3). The Arab-Israeli conflict will be resolved. The Western dictator (the beast out of the sea—Revelation 13:1-10) will succeed temporarily in bringing order out of chaos. The Jewish antichrist (the beast out of the earth—Revelation 13:11-18) will succeed in restoring economic prosperity. Perhaps the nations will sign pledges to ban armaments. The age-long dream for global tranquility will seem to materialize. But Egypt will invade Palestine. Russia will retaliate, the Western Allies will be drawn into the contest, and the armies of the Orient will cross the Euphrates into the Mideast.

Israel will become the battleground on which the superpowers fight. The holocaust will result in awful destruction of life and property. Israel will be seized with birth pangs. She will suffer bitter anguish in that hour of her greatest peril, but out of the travail God will bring into existence a spiritual Israel to whom He can and will fulfill the promises made to the fathers. God intends to reduce Israel to such drastic straits that she will have no other option than to call for the Lord Jesus to come save her from genocide.

THE DAY OF DELIVERANCE
(I Thessalonians 5:4-11)

That terrible day of affliction will not catch true Christians unaware (verse 4). They belong to the period of the day of Christ, not the day of the Lord. They anticipate the day of resurrection, the day of rapture, the day of reunion, the day of rejoicing. Because they have been translated out of the kingdom of darkness, they have no part or portion in the coming "day of darkness and gloominess, a day of clouds and of thick darkness" (Joel 2:2). They are the possessors of intellectual, moral, and spiritual light (I Thessalonians 5:5). They walk and work in the light. "All" the church saints are the sons of light—even those who need correction; consequently, all believers of

Colossians 1:13

the church age will be spared the period of gross darkness—the tribulation.

The sons of light are not immune to seasons of drowsiness. They can become negligent and indifferent to the dangers that lurk at noonday. They might grow weary of waiting for Christ to come and relax their vigil. The flesh is weak. Nothing is easier than dropping off to sleep, but remaining awake when you are tired requires real effort. Therefore, Paul urged that we all remain alert (verse 6). The hours of the day are fast waning. It is no time even for a catnap. The days are evil; we must buy up the opportunities while it is day.

Paul exhorted the Christians at Rome to "awake out of sleep" (Romans 13:11).

Ephesians 5:16

The people of Noah's day passed the hours eating and drinking. Gluttony and drunkenness marked their behavior. For them, life consisted of self-indulgence, spiritual stupor, and sexual excesses. They rode the merry-go-round of pleasure without any consciousness that amusements would be terminated by a universal judgment. So, the people of our generation are staggering under the influence of worldly ambition, materialism, and fleshly pleasure (verse 7). Many are drunk with power. Some are sedated to torpor; others are stimulated to unnatural excitability. But all belong to the period of darkness and will be swept away with the wicked.

The Christian maintains his spiritual health by taking necessary precautions. He arms himself with faith in God, love toward others, and hope in deliverance (verse 8). Love is his insurance against spiritual heart trouble. Hope is a precaution against psychoses and neuroses. The world scene already indicates that the night of social and political chaos is pending, but the Christian is a bulwark of optimism because he knows that the

Paul refers again to the armor in Romans 13:12; II Corinthians 6:7; Ephesians 6:11-13.

day of final redemption is nigh.

Not only that, the child of God knows that he will not be called upon to enter the period when God will pour out the vials of His wrath (verse 9). The Christian's lot is to experience a deliverance from the day of vengeance and not a deliverance in the midst of it or through it. The church has an appointment in the skies. Various groups of saints have their specific appointments according to the purposes of God. The tribulation has no purpose to serve as far as the church saints are concerned; it has a dramatic role to play, however, in the purposes of God for Israel and the Gentile nations.

The substitutionary work of Christ at Calvary is the ground of present and prospective salvation (verse 10). Because Christ died on our behalf and in our place, we have the blessed assurance of being in His company forever. He has rescued us already from the dominion of sin. He has endured the full brunt of God's wrath against sin, so we shall never experience it. He will release the dead saints from the power of physical death, and He will rescue us who are living from the jaws of the tribulation.

Such good news ought to prompt Christians to encourage eath other in these days of ecclesiastical, social, political, military, educational, and moral upheaval (verse 11). Let's engage in a constructive ministry of building each other up in the most holy faith while we are waiting for Jesus to snatch us out of tribulation danger.

The New Testament distinguishes three classes of people: Jews, Gentiles, and the church. The church consists of saved Jews and Gentiles who are added to the body of Christ and thus lose their racial distinctions (Galatians 3:28).

FOOD FOR THOUGHT

"Don't curse the darkness—light a candle."

—Chinese Proverb

NOW TEST YOUR KNOWLEDGE

Answer true or false:

1. "The day of the Lord" and "the day of Christ" refer to two different occasions. ____
2. We have warrant for making reasonable guesses about the time of Christ's return. ____
3. Israel will benefit from the troubles of the tribulation. ____
4. A short-lived period of peace will precede the destruction of the day of the Lord. ____
5. God's appointments for the saints of all the ages vary according to His purpose. ____
6. The tribulation will serve to purify church saints. ____
7. Other periods in history have been as terrible as the day of the Lord will be. ____

LAST-MINUTE INSTRUCTIONS

LESSON SCRIPTURE
I Thessalonians 5:12-28

RELATED SCRIPTURES
I Corinthians 3:1-23;
Colossians 4:7-18

LESSON AIM
To advance in Christian development through the appropriation of God-appointed means.

LEARN BY HEART
"And the very God of peace sanctify you wholly; and I pray God your whole spirit and soul and body be preserved blameless unto the coming of our Lord Jesus Christ" (I Thessalonians 5:23).

EVERY DAY WITH THE WORD

STUDENT'S NOTEBOOK

This column is for the student who desires additional study of the lesson theme.

Monday	Predawn prayer	Psalm 119:145-152
Tuesday	Morning prayer	Psalm 5:1-7
Wednesday	Noon prayer	Psalm 55:16-23
Thursday	Evening prayer	Acts 3:1-11
Friday	Night prayer	Psalm 42:1-8
Saturday	Midnight prayer	Acts 16:25-29
Sunday	Continual prayer	Ephesians 6:18-24

LESSON PREPARATION

Watch out for three subtle forms of pride: pride of face, pride of race, and pride of grace. Some

A rather pompous-looking deacon was endeavoring to impress on a class of young boys the importance of living the Christian life. "Why do people call me a Christian?" the dignitary asked, standing very erect and beaming down upon them.

After a moment's pause, one of the youngsters ventured a guess: "It may be because they don't know you."

Something of the same situation was brewing at Thessalonica. The church officers had been taking steps to correct unruly members and impose upon them certain principles of Christian living. The members tended to resist admonition and resent the authority of the leaders. Their attitudes and actions related to an ignorance of and unappreciation for the men whom God had appointed to shepherd them. These deficiencies moved Paul to write some final instructions to the saints at Thessalonica.

people are proud of their spiritual attainments.

The Thessalonians were not perfect (I Thessalonians 3:10).

INSTRUCTIONS ABOUT CHRISTIAN DUTY (I Thessalonians 5:12-22)

The members of a local church should get to know their spiritual leaders in the sense of becoming more aware and appreciative of their vital ministry in the church. Doubtlessly, the church at Thessalonica had early followed the practice of the other churches by electing church officers, and these men were a credit to the ministry. They were laborers, not loiterers; leaders, not dictators. They presided over the local church, maintained order, and expostulated with any saint who stepped out of line (verse 12).

Note the duty of members toward the leaders (I Corinthians 16:10,11; Philippians 2:29,30; Hebrews 13:7,17,24).

God's ministers are worthy of respect and affection not because of who they are but because of what God has called them to do (verse 13). We honor them "for their work's sake." It is not enough for the people to acknowledge the pastor and deacons with reluctance or regard their posi-

Observe the
qualifications of
a bishop in
I Timothy 3:1-11.

Consider various
injunctions about
peace (Romans
12:18; II Corin-
thians 13:11;
Colossians 3:15).

tion as a necessary evil. The Word of God calls for attitudes of love and loyalty toward Christian leaders. It goes without saying, however, that these men should behave in such a manner as to be worthy of the saints' confidence in them. Love and loyalty should characterize the pastor as well as the people. This relationship will create an atmosphere of peace in the church. Mutual regard will solve most problems in the local assembly.

The delinquent or defective saint should be the concern of all (verse 14). The loafers need to be prodded to action. The Scriptural invitations to rest do not include a disorderly idleness in which a lazy Christian imposes upon others for his keep. Truants from work had better return to the job. Likewise, someone will have to encourage faint-hearted Christians. They entertain a dread of persecution, a sense of personal failure, a fear of the future, a grief over the death of loved ones. Everything discourages them. Timorous and lily-livered, they give up easily and back off from every confrontation. Nevertheless, they belong to Christ, and more spiritual Christians are responsible for their care.

Speaking by divine authority, Paul forbids the practice of personal retaliation among Christians (verse 15). They must never pay back a dirty deed with a dirty deed. Vengeance is the sole prerogative of God; therefore, any believer who seeks redress or revenge is usurping God's role. It is enough for us to know that God will vindicate us in His own good time. Meanwhile, let's not butt into God's business.

Consider also
Romans 12:17-21.

Remember, David
would not take
any action
against Saul
even though the
king made
repeated
attempts upon
David's life.

On the negative side, the Christian refuses to settle accounts with those who make life miserable for him. He harbors no resentment or rankle. On the positive side, he pursues the good. He persistently moves in the direction of that which will prove helpful both to his enemies and to his friends. Every contact a Christian has with other people should leave them better persons for having been in his company.

Not only is the Christian to forgive his foes and benefit others, he is to do it joyfully (verse 16). If you say you forgive someone and then make that person feel that you deserve special credit for it, you have not fulfilled the Biblical ideal. Or, if you say, "I forgive you, but I'll never forget it," you have not really forgiven. Or, if you bear injuries with a stoic resignation, a martyr complex, or a sour disposition, you have not entered into the joy of forgiving others.

Find reasons for joy in the following verses: John 4:36; Acts 11:23; Romans 15:32; I Corinthians 16:17; II Corinthians 7:9; Colossians 2:5; Philemon 7; Hebrews 10:34; III John 3,4.

Every experience of the believer's life is an occasion for gladness. Even unpleasant events cannot diminish the deep-seated joy of those whose hope and happiness are fixed on Christ. Such joy is independent of circumstances—good or bad; it is the effect of the Spirit of joy working in the human emotions.

Laboring, supervising, loving, comforting, forgiving, and rejoicing all relate to praying (verse 17). Prayer is an acknowledgement that we are incapable on our own of measuring up even in part to God's requirements for us. We must have supernatural assistance in order to perform spiritual exercises, and so we go continually to God and ask for it. Prayer is our lifeline to Heaven's resources. Prevailing prayer brings perpetual power.

James 5:16

Someone once said, "A coffee break is good; a prayer break is better; a praise break is best." Paul said, "In every thing give thanks" (verse 18).

There is no exception to that rule. We rejoice no matter what the circumstance, we pray about everything, and we voice our gratitude to God for whatever He brings into our experience. Nothing merely happens. God is working out His sovereign plan in our lives, and we must respond by giving Him thanks. This is an aspect of His will which He has disclosed in His Son, our Saviour.

Each Christian is supposed to be fervent in spirit and not suppress the ardor which the Spirit is working in either him or in others (verse 19). Stifling the impulses which the Holy Spirit produces in the soul is a sin against Him. When the Spirit moves us to pray, witness, exhort, sing, or even shout "amen," we must not quench the fire which He has kindled in us. When he activates someone else to preach, regardless of who it is, we must be receptive to the message (verse 20).

On the other hand, not all impulses come from the Holy Spirit. Other spirits are influencing the souls of men, exiting them to fleshly joy, boistrous and disruptive conduct in church meetings, and fanatical enthusiasm. We need to be certain that our impulses originate from the Spirit's prompting, and so we must "prove all things" (verse 21). We have to test the stirrings which come to us in order to decide their origin. The measuring rod is the Word of God. The Holy Spirit will never move a child of God to do anything contrary to the Word of God.

INSTRUCTIONS ABOUT CHRISTIAN DEVELOPMENT (I Thessalonians 5:23-28)

Paul had already instructed the Thessalonians

Romans 12:11

Believers may commit three sins against the Spirit: quenching, grieving, and lying to Him.

I John 4:1

about several vital aspects of sanctification, and now at the conclusion of his remarks he returned to this important subject. He prayed that God would sanctify them "wholly"—that is, in the totality of their being (verse 23). It does not mean that believers will experience eradication of indwelling sin or that we shall experience "entire sanctification" in this life. It does mean that progressively the Holy Spirit will invade the citadel of the soul, infusing His own moral qualities in us and restraining those propensities which we received from Adam.

Eradication of sin is the experience only of the disembodied condition or the glorified state. In our present experience we never reach the point at which we cannot sin or do not sin.

Using as His headquarters the human spirit, in which He dwells, the Holy Spirit conducts supernatural operations in the field of the soul. The result is that He preserves and purifies both the spirit and the soul which in turn have their effect in bringing the members of the physical body into subservience to righteousness. At the coming of the Lord the work will be complete. As long as believers live in an unglorified state, however, the soul is the battleground where the Holy Spirit and the principle of indwelling sin engage in a relentless struggle for the conquest of every facet of the believer's complex personality.

Romans 7:23; Galatians 5:17; I Peter 2:11

The work of sanctification is sure (verse 24). Every Christian without exception experiences it—some to a greater degree than others. Those whom God justifies, He sanctifies. There is no such thing as justification without sanctification. The God who called us to salvation has pledged also to work in us by the Holy Spirit in order to produce in us those godly virtues which He demands of us. In sanctifying power God will and does infuse a spiritual joy into our emotions, a hatred for sin in all its forms, an attitude of gratitude, a spirit of

Romans 8:29

The Holy Spirit could no more abandon His purpose to make us holy than the Lord Jesus could abandon His purpose to save us.

forgiveness, and whatever else He requires. He also works in our minds and wills so that we are receptive and responsive to His mind and will.

But these ministries also depend upon our appropriation of certain God-appointed means. Prayer (verse 25), fellowship (verse 26), and Scripture (verse 27) are the means God uses to sanctify us progressively. The process of sanctification and the means to attain it work together. If, however, the believer were left entirely to himself, he would never appropriate the means. Therefore, God graciously moves him to lay hold of the means. In other words, the sanctifying influences of the Holy Spirit at work in us cause us to love to pray, read God's Word, and fellowship with others of like precious faith.

Early in the church's history holy "brethren" exchanged a "holy kiss" (verse 26). The men kissed the men, and the women kissed the women as an expression of spiritual love for each other. But this form of greeting soon suffered abuse with the result that it was abandoned. Today it is customary and appropriate for people to extend a hearty handshake instead.

Peter calls it "a kiss of charity [love]" (I Peter 5:14).

God leaves nothing to chance in His mighty operations and eternal purpose to conform us to the image of the Lord Jesus. All that He accomplishes in us by these omnipotent exercises in our whole being must be traced to God's amazing Grace (verse 28), and the gracious work will continue until we stand in His presence blameless and faultless.

FOOD FOR THOUGHT

"He who has the Holy Spirit in his heart and the Scripture in his hands has all he needs."

—Alexander Maclaren

NOW TEST YOUR KNOWLEDGE

Answer in your own words:

1. In what way are we supposed to "know" our church officers? _____

2. Why should members of local churches esteem their Christian leaders? _____

3. What will solve most problems in the local assembly? _____

4. Who is responsible to care for the weaker Christians? _____

5. Why is personal revenge wrong? _____

6. What kind of forgiveness does the Lord demand? _____

7. Under what circumstances should we be thankful? _____

8. What does it mean to "quench" the Spirit? _____

9. How can we decide the origin of our impulses? __

10. What are the means for attaining sanctification? _____ , _____ , _____

FOR TROUBLOUS TIMES

10

LESSON SCRIPTURE
II Thessalonians 1:1-12

RELATED SCRIPTURE
The Book of I Peter

LESSON AIM
To comfort Christians who are
persecuted.

LEARN BY HEART
"Wherefore let them that suffer according to the will of God commit
the keeping of their souls to him in
well doing, as unto a faithful
Creator" (I Peter 4:19).

EVERY DAY WITH THE WORD

STUDENT'S NOTEBOOK

This column is for
the student who
desires additional
study of the lesson
theme.

Monday	Increased joy	Isaiah 29:17-24
Tuesday	Increased numbers	Acts 6:1-7
Wednesday	Increased strength	Acts 9:17-25
Thursday	Increased fruit	II Corinthians 9:6-15
Friday	Increased faith	II Corinthians 10:12-18
Saturday	Increased knowledge	Colossians 1:9-14
Sunday	Increased love	I Thessalonians 4:1-12

LESSON PREPARATION

"Many waters
cannot quench
love, neither can
the floods drown
it: if a man would
give all the

One young man spent the whole evening telling
his girl friend how much he loved her. He said that
he would never be able to live without her, that he
would go to the ends of the earth for her, that he
would go through fire and flood for her and even

81

die for her. But when he was leaving, he said, "I'll see you tomorrow night if it doesn't rain."

If rain can keep a fellow away from a girl he says he loves, we have good reason for doubting the genuineness of his profession. Likewise, if the commonplace trials of this life can keep Christians away from abiding in Christ, we have cause to suspect the reality of their conversion.

substance of his house for love, it would utterly be contemned" (Song of Solomon 8:7).

STEADFASTNESS IN PERSECUTION
(II Thessalonians 1:1-4)

The steadfastness of the Thessalonians despite increasing persecution provided one of the proofs that they had really passed from death to life. Apparently they thought that the dread period of the tribulation had come upon them, yet still they held fast to Christ and patiently bore their troubles.

Many factors entered into their fortitude. First of all, they had the encouragement of the evangelists who were responsible under God for founding the work at Thessalonica (verse 1). Paul, Silas, and Timothy kept the communication lines open with them. Paul corresponded with them, and Silas and Timothy conveyed letters and brought back reports. Christian workers always play a large part in how the congregation of the saints react to trials.

We dare not be indifferent to the needs of God's people.

More importantly, however, believers are able to stand for God because they enjoy an intimate relationship with the Godhead. Christians are "in God . . . and the Lord Jesus Christ." This involves a life-sustaining union. As the branch is in the vine and drawing its life from the vine, so believers are in Christ and receiving sustaining grace from Him. Abiding in Christ results in the

John 15:1-21

fruit of perseverance.

Grace and peace also contribute to our endurance (verse 2). God graciously strengthens us for the conflict, and we rest in the reconciling work of Christ on our behalf. We are no longer estranged from God; God is working mightily in us to preserve us from falling. The fact that Jesus Christ acts jointly with the Father in bestowing upon believers the grace of persistence and the peace of God indirectly proves that He is God, for He participates in divine activities.

How many times in the New Testament do you find grace and peace associated with the Father and the Son?

These truths are more than an occasion for giving thanks to God; they constitute an obligation to give thanks (verse 3). To say "Thank You" is a debt we owe God for His part in causing our faith to grow, our love to abound, and our patience to endure. It is only appropriate to be grateful to the One who creates and cultivates these spiritual virtues in us. God must have the praise because He is the causal source of all and any good that is in us.

God works in us that which is well-pleasing in His sight (Hebrews 13:21).

So extraordinary was the behavior of the Thessalonian Christians toward God and their fellow believers that Paul could not restrain himself from feeling a godly pride in them (verse 4). He took pleasure in informing the churches, especially in Achaia and Macedonia, of the exploits of the saints at Thessalonica. They exhibited unusual qualities, but God got the credit for it. When Paul boasted about them, he boasted in God's grace which produced the exceptional effects.

Paul also had a godly jealousy over his converts (II Corinthians 11:2).

The fires of persecution cannot persuade a truly regenerate person to abandon his faith in Christ. We are by no means consistently and continually triumphant. We often take a temporary turn for the worse and in a moment deny the Lord or give

Persecution purifies genuine faith (I Peter 1:6,7).

place to the devil. Periods of weakness and spiritual decline overtake all Christians, but God ultimately intervenes to check our drifting, strengthen our faith, and establish our goings. When faith is strong, steadfastness follows. Indeed, an active resistance to the temptation to defect and a perseverance to go on with the Lord are some of the surest signs of spiritual life.

The persistence in view here is the kind which holds steady when no immediate end of troubles is in sight. Paul did not promise the Thessalonians that their suffering would cease in this life. Trouble will continue, but God's sustaining grace will always be sufficient.

II Corinthians 12:9

SOLACE IN PERSECUTION
(II Thessalonians 1:5-12)

We must never regard suffering for righteousness' sake as an experience to be dreaded and avoided. Often trouble is God's means of stabilizing our faith. He has His own good and sufficient reasons for permitting the enemy of our souls to harass us and for allowing unbelievers to heckle us. God is righteous in all of His wise decisions, and when He chooses to give us a taste of trouble, we must not resent His methods of dealing with us (verse 5). A bitter spirit may indicate that we are not yet suited for participation in the millennial reign. It is the plain teaching of God's Word that we shall enter the kingdom through many trials. The trials gain for us no merit. We shall not reign with Christ because we deserve to. Nothing we are, do, or believe gives us a claim on such a privilege. But sufferings are an avenue to the king-

Matthew 5:10

God sent a messenger of Satan to buffet Paul (II Corinthians 12:7).

Acts 14:22

dom. We cannot arrive in the kingdom without journeying over the highways of trouble.

It is important to understand what Paul meant by "the kingdom of God." Bible teachers have suggested all sorts of possibilities. They explain it as the realm of salvation, the sphere of grace, the sovereignty of God, the invisible church, the Christian dispensation, the community of those who own the Lordship of Christ, the development of God's cause among men, or Heaven itself. None of these explanations is adequate. The New Testament will make a whole lot more sense to you if you will think of every reference to the kingdom in terms of the millennial kingdom.

Perhaps the church's relationship to the kingdom of God needs clarification. In I Thessalonians 2:12 we learned that the church is being called "unto" that kingdom. In II Thessalonians 1:5 we discover that the church is being fitted for that kingdom. Acts 28:23,31 suggests that the coming kingdom is a proper subject for teaching and preaching. The saints of the church age are destined to inherit the kingdom (Galatians 5:21; Ephesians 5:5; James 2:5). Our participation is so certain that God considers us to be in it before its historical fulfillment (Colossians 1:13).

We are working "unto the kingdom"—that is, laboring with the kingdom in view (Colossians 4:11). The church will be the ruling aristocracy during the period of the kingdom (II Timothy 2:12). We are being preserved now for that kingdom (II Timothy 4:18). We shall have an abundant entrance into that kingdom when at last it has its historical realization (II Peter 1:11). The church saints suffer tribulation because they are patiently waiting for Jesus to come and set up that

We recognize also the universal government of God in which God rules throughout all time and in all spheres over all beings, but the term "kingdom of God" does not refer to the universal government of God.

Commenting on the references to the "kingdom" in the New Testament epistles, A. J. McClain says, ". . . There is not one which grammatically cannot be interpreted consistently with the doctrine of a future kingdom."

kingdom on the earth (Revelation 1:9).

When troubles roll over us like ocean billows, we have to remember that in God's good time He will dispense judgment on those who try to make life miserable for us (II Thessalonians 1:6). Whatever God does is just and fair. If He acquits sinners, He is just in doing so and thus manifests His grace and mercy. If He condemns sinners, He is also just and thus displays His severity. Goodness and severity belong to God's essential character, and He will have proper objects on which He can exercise both—His goodness on those who lay claim to the provisions of Calvary and His wrath upon those who repudiate God's proffer of mercy in Christ.

While we are waiting for God to right the wrongs and restore justice in the earth, let's "rest" (verse 7). We have no reason for being, as they say, "uptight." The pressures of persecution need not stretch us emotionally taut. Let's relax when the blows come; they won't hurt nearly so much. Then, in due time, Christ will intervene by His personal presence to vindicate the right and revenge the wrong. He will dispatch the angels of His power to execute judgment upon the ungodly.

Certainly we must not take Job's attitude and wish that we were dead (Job 3:11-17). Rather, we look all the more earnestly for Christ to come (James 5:7,8).

The gospel calls upon sinners to turn from their sins and cordially embrace the Lord Jesus as their Saviour. Their refusal to do so renders them fully responsible and culpable for their unbelief (verse 8). They will be sentenced to eternal perdition not because they are nonelect but because they resolved to reject what Christ did for them at Calvary.

John 3:17-21; 3:36

The cults are determined to eliminate the doctrine of eternal punishment from the Bible. They explain it away in a variety of ways, but texts like

Jesus taught the doctrine of

eternal
punishment
(Mark 9:43-48).

verse 9 continue to haunt them. "Everlasting destruction" is the exact opposite of "eternal life." If what we get in Christ is an endless joy, then those who are not in Christ must suffer endless judgment. If the one experience is without cessation, so must the other be. Sinners will exist in a state of conscious torment, banished from the face of Christ forever and forever.

The coming of Christ will make all of the sufferings of this life well worthwhile. Because we suffer for Him, we shall reign with Him. When He appears, we shall appear with Him in glory. He has always amazed us with His marvelous, infinite, matchless grace; but when He appears in splendor in the skies, we shall be dazzled by His glory and power (verse 10). The saints will thrill at His presence and glory in His procession to the earth, when He will remove sinners to a place of interminable woe and welcome saints to the era of millennial glory.

Colossians 3:4

I Peter 4:13;
5:1,4,10

Whether that day is near or distant, we do not know for sure. If the time is short, we shall suffer only briefly. If the time is long, we need an unfailing supply of sustaining grace and keeping power. And for this we have every warrant and need to pray (verse 11). Knowing the insufficiencies of any power that derives from us, we must call upon God to fill us with a desire and with the power to do good, to do works indicative of our faith, to prove ourselves worthy by grace of our calling.

"Now for a
season" (I Peter
1:6).

The power is not
"of us" (II Corin-
thians 4:7).
Without Christ
we can do
nothing (John
15:5). "Our
sufficiency is of
God" (II Corin-
thians 3:5).

God purposes that Christ will be glorified whether by our life or our death. We are Christ's masterpiece, and we shall show Him off in the day that He puts us on display as the trophies of His grace (verse 12). All that He has done for us, through us, and in us will redound to His eternal credit. His grace has made us what we are, and what we shall yet be will cause the saints and angels to exalt the precious name of Jesus.

FOOD FOR THOUGHT

"Great works are performed, not by strength but by perseverance."
—Samuel Johnson

NOW TEST YOUR KNOWLEDGE

Match the terms by putting letters in the blanks:

1. ____ Charity	A.	Affliction
2. ____ Destruction	B.	Boast
3. ____ Everlasting	C.	Endless
4. ____ Faith	D.	Fair
5. ____ Glory	E.	Love
6. ____ Kingdom	F.	Millennium
7. ____ Patience	G.	Perseverance
8. ____ Peace	H.	Reconciliation
9. ____ Rest	I.	Relaxation
10. ____ Righteous	J.	Revenge
11. ____ Tribulation	K.	Ruination
12. ____ Vengeance	L.	Trust

THE DAY OF DREAD AND DOOM

11

LESSON SCRIPTURE
II Thessalonians 2:1-12

RELATED SCRIPTURE
Daniel 11:36-39; Revelation 13:11-18

LESSON AIM
To work and witness as the rapture approaches.

LEARN BY HEART
"Let no man deceive you by any means: for that day shall not come, except there come a falling away first, and that man of sin be revealed, the son of perdition"
(II Thessalonians 2:3).

EVERY DAY WITH THE WORD

STUDENT'S NOTEBOOK

This column is for the student who desires additional study of the lesson theme.

Monday	The refuge of lies	Isaiah 28:14-20
Tuesday	The profane prince	Ezekiel 21:25-32
Wednesday	The willful king	Daniel 11:36-39
Thursday	The idol shepherd	Zechariah 11:7-17
Friday	The hireling	John 10:7-14
Saturday	The antichrist	II John 7-11
Sunday	The earth-beast	Revelation 13:11-18

LESSON PREPARATION

II Timothy 1:12

As the great Biblical scholar, Bengel, lay on his deathbed, one of his friends quoted, or rather misquoted, a well-known verse of Scripture, adding the word "in" where it did not belong: "I know in whom I have believed."

89

"No, no," said the dying believer, "do not allow even a preposition to come between my Saviour and me: 'I know whom I have believed'!"

We all make mistakes in our quoting, understanding, and applying of Scripture. Fortunate is the person who has a friend better versed than he, who will point out the error and endeavor to correct him. This was the relationship between the Apostle Paul and the Thessalonians. They entertained some misconceptions about the Lord's return, and Paul was faithful to set them on the path of truth again.

Paul had the sad duty to correct Peter (Galatians 2:11), but Peter did not resent it (II Peter 3:15,16).

DECEPTION CONCERNING THE DAY OF THE LORD (II Thessalonians 2:1-5)

Somehow the Thessalonians had been convinced that the dreaded day of the Lord had already dawned in history. Paul speculated that the source of the error may have derived from "spirit"—that is, a purported disclosure directly from the Holy Spirit to someone in the congregation. Or, perhaps the saints misconstrued something Paul had spoken when he was with them. The error may also have come from a letter forged with Paul's name. At any rate, the Thessalonians lived in a state of mental agitation and emotional unbalance as the result of believing a false report, and Paul considered it his duty to rectify their mistaken notions.

The "discerning of spirits" was an extraordinary gift which the Holy Spirit bestowed upon certain believers in the first-century church (I Corinthians 12:10).

Many practical truths appear in verses 1-5. In verse 1, note that the truth of the coming of Christ provides an appropriate basis on which we may plead with others to forsake error and embrace the truth. In view of the imminent appearing of the Lord, we have plenty of reason to correct false

How often in the Thessalonian epistles can you find practical behavior related to the truth of the Lord's return?

teaching. When errors arise, we should take the initiative to challenge them. In passing, also observe that the coming of the Lord consists of "our gathering together." Christ will muster His troops and assemble the saints in the skies. Finally, consider that the believer should look not for the coming of antichrist but for the coming of Christ. He is our hope and the single object of our interest. We have every right to be occupied with the truth of His coming, but we must not entertain false ideas about it.

From verse 2 we infer that believers are often too hasty in their conclusions. The Thessalonians were "soon" unsettled. We must learn to exercise a holy criticism. The ability to discern truth from error is a mark of Christian maturity. We cannot afford to be gullible, for false teachers abound today. An experience of regeneration does not render us immune from being deceived and disturbed. We need a continual fortification of our minds with sound doctrine if we hope to maintain our theological equilibrium.

Verse 3 suggests that Satan has more than one means of deceiving the people of God. His devices are many. He employs the services of false teachers and perpetuates error by perverting the very words of Scripture. The devil can quote Scripture to his own advantage. We can also deduce from this verse the truth that each one of us is responsible before God not to be deceived. Even though the serpent beguiled Eve, God judged Eve. "Be not deceived" is a divine order. No matter how ignorantly we succumb, we are still guilty.

Has anyone ever asked you whether you thought that the church was already in the tribula-

Ephesians 4:14-16; I John 4:1

II Peter 2:1-3

Genesis 3:16; I Timothy 2:14

tion period? How would you prove that we are not in the tribulation? Paul gave a ready answer to the same problem. He said that people would recognize the tribulation by the arrival of an unprecedented apostasy and by the revelation of the personal antichrist. Neither of these events has occurred yet, and so we can be sure that we are not in the tribulation period. In fact, neither of these events will occur until the church has been raptured to glory.

The "falling away" signifies something more than general apostasy in the church. Almost as soon as the church was born, false teachers began their work of perverting the truth, but all of the heretical teachings during the church age do not signal the arrival of the day of the Lord. Some unique apostasy must be in view. In all likelihood it refers to *the* transgression of Israel when the apostate nation consents to the reintroduction of idolatry in the land. The apostasy and the revelation of the antichrist—the man of sin—go hand in hand.

Jesus spoke of the spread of false prophets (Matthew 24:23-27).

The antichrist will direct religious worship during the last half of the tribulation period. He will sit in the reconstructed Jewish temple as a priest. He will receive divine honors and titles. He will direct worship toward the European dictator and also toward himself. The antichrist will introduce the final form of man-made religion—a religion which deifies man and defies God.

Daniel 11:38; Revelation 13:12

DISCLOSURES ABOUT THE DAY OF THE LORD (II Thessalonians 2:6-12)

Paul mentioned several truths that pertained to the day of the Lord: 1) something or someone is presently holding in check the unparalleled wickedness that will characterize the tribulation period; 2) during the tribulation iniquity will abound, but it will not abide because Christ will come to destroy the forces of evil; 3) those who identify themselves with the antichrist by receiving his mark will share his eternal fate in the Lake of Fire. These facts are the main import of verses 6-12, but let us study this passage also for the purpose of gleaning applicable principles.

Note that the second beast of Revelation gives the mark (13:16).

First, we learn that wickedness cannot break out by its own sovereign will; it always lies under restrictions, limitations, and control. Not until an omnipotent power removes the restraints can the forces of iniquity exercise their will and way. At the present time wickedness is working in the world, but its force and effect are nothing compared to what they will be when God lifts His restraining hand, for then lawlessness will run rampant. Unregenerate men, demons, and Satan cannot now pursue all the bents of their evil natures, for God the Spirit holds the reins upon them; but the day will come when the Holy Spirit will relax the reins and allow the wicked to follow the natural course of their depraved inclinations.

Lawlessness will be promoted by the lawless one. Twice in this passage (verses 3,7) Paul uses the word *anomia* and once he uses the word *anomos* (verse 8) to emphasize the character of the tribulation era: in verse 3, "man of sin" should be rendered "the lawless one"; in verse 7, "iniquity" is literally "the lawlessness"; and in verse 8, "that Wicked" is more correctly "the lawless one." The spirit of antichrist is the spirit of lawlessness, and those who break the law of God or violate civil law partake of the nature of the coming antichrist. The

From the Greek prefix *a-* (no) and *nomos* (law), meaning "without law."

Expositors are not in agreement about the antichrist, but these

93

unprecedented wave of anarchy across the world today is preparing the way for the antichrist.

The antichrist will be revealed in his time and also ruined at the appointed time. Christ will deal personally with the antichrist and his colleague, the Roman prince of Europe. At the end of the tribulation both the beast (the European dictator) and the false prophet (the Jewish antichrist) will be cast alive into the lake of fire; and after a thousand years—after the millennial reign—both will still be suffering the torments of perdition.

That the antichrist is a prophet as well as a priest and king is clear from verse 9. The Lord Jesus vindicated His right to the prophetic office by performing miracles. The false christ will likewise perform miracles to persuade the Jews that he is the prophet like Moses whom God promised to raise up (compare Deuteronomy 18:18 and Revelation 13:13). In every respect the devil's christ will imitate the Christ of God. He will pose as a lamb but in reality be a wild beast. He will do great wonders after the fashion of Elijah but will be, nevertheless, a false prophet. He will seem to give life to the image of the first beast, thereby aping the life-giving Christ. He will identify his own with a mark, just as Christ seals His own with the Holy Spirit. He will feed those who own him, just as Christ fed the multitudes who came to Him. He will depend upon supernatural help to perform miracles and receive that power from the devil, just as Christ performed many of His miracles by the Spirit of God—a supernatural assistant.

All of the wonderwork of the antichrist will be calculated to deceive those who perish. By miracles he will persuade them to believe lies. The

lessons follow the identification of Scofield as given in note 3, pages 1342, 1343, of the *Scofield Reference Bible*.

Revelation 13:15

Revelation 13:16
Revelation 13:17

miracles of Christ, on the other hand, were designed to convince men of the truth. What a tragic commentary that unregenerate men are easily persuaded by Satanic miracles to believe falsehood but are unmoved by Holy Spirit miracles to believe the truth!

The miracles of the antichrist will be real and energized by Satan—like the miracles which Pharaoh's magicians performed in Egypt.

In verse 10 we have an emphatic declaration that in order to be saved men must "receive the love of the truth." The reason that people will not receive the truth is that they hate it. We are readily parted from that for which we have no love. Whoever refuses the truth adopts the attitude of the antichrist and will share in his ruin.

Because sinful men will not welcome the truth, God will send a delusion upon them (verse 11—literally, a working of error). When God puts forth His power, the unrighteous will believe the lie. God will deliver them over to the falsehoods in which they think to find safety and security. God will use their sin of unbelief as an occasion to punish them and at the same time vindicate His righteousness.

Unbelievers also hate those who tell them the truth (John 8:40).

Men naturally hate the truth which God sends to them for their salvation; they have an aversion to it in their hearts. But instead of destroying them at once, by a powerful divine operation God takes definite steps to bring to the surface all of the innate sin and madness of their hearts; and He does it in order to bring sinners to judgment and in order that He shall be justified when He speaks condemnation and banishes them to Hell (verse 12).

God will bring the antichrist on the scene in order to demonstrate that, given the right circumstances and freed from divine restraints, men will infallibly exercise a spontaneous and free will to despise God's saving grace and give ready assent to the lies of the bloody and deceitful antichrist.

FOOD FOR THOUGHT

"A man should never be ashamed to own he has been in the wrong, which is but saying, in other words, that he is wiser today than he was yesterday."

—Alexander Pope

NOW TEST YOUR KNOWLEDGE

Give short answers:

1. What names does Scripture give to the antichrist?
   _____, _____, _____,
   _____, _____, _____.
2. Who will empower the antichrist to perform miracles? _____
3. Identify the restrainer. _____
4. What sources may have convinced the Thessalonians that the day of the Lord had already come?
   _____, _____, _____.
5. In what sense will the Holy Spirit be taken out of the way? _____.
6. What must a person do in order to be saved? ____
   _____.
7. What two events will indicate that the tribulation is already in progress? _____
   _____ and _____.

EVERYTHING BY PRAYER AND THANKSGIVING

12

LESSON SCRIPTURE
II Thessalonians 2:13—3:5

RELATED SCRIPTURE
Matthew 6:9-13; Ephesians 1:4;
I Peter 1:2

LESSON AIM
To pray for the successful proc-
lamation of the Word of God.

LEARN BY HEART
"Finally, brethren, pray for us, that
the word of the Lord may have free
course, and be glorified, even as it
is with you" (II Thessalonians 3:1).

EVERY DAY WITH THE WORD

STUDENT'S NOTEBOOK

This column is for
the student who
desires additional
study of the lesson
theme.

Monday	Hold fast his integrity	Job 2:18
Tuesday	Hold fast the good	I Thessalonians 5:14-28
Wednesday	Hold fast the Word	Titus 1:7-16
Thursday	Hold fast sound words	II Timothy 1:8-14
Friday	Hold fast the confidence	Hebrews 3:1-6
Saturday	Hold fast the profession	Hebrews 10:19-25
Sunday	Hold fast my name	Revelation 2:12-17

LESSON PREPARATION

The Christian on
his knees sees
more than the
philosopher on
tiptoe (Toplady).

A wise man said, "If stress and strife of the
times cause us to become weak-kneed, perhaps we
should let them collapse entirely and while in that
position do a little serious praying." This was the
Apostle Paul's experience. The description which

he gave in II Thessalonians 2:3-12 of the antichrist and his followers drove him to prayer. He could not help thinking about the character, career, and destiny of the wicked as compared with the spiritual blessings of the child of God both for time and eternity. Paul responded to these realities by offering a prayer of praise and a prayer of petition.

THE PRAYER OF PRAISE
(II Thessalonians 2:13-17)

That we should escape the doom awaiting the antichrist and all the wicked is reason for praise and thanks to God. There was a time in our lives when we too lived according to the course of this world and were by nature the children of wrath. If we received what our sins deserved, we would suffer the same fate as the antichrist. What made the difference? God from eternity past had planned to apply the benefits of the atonement to our unworthy souls, deliver us from the tyranny of our sins, and recreate us in the image of Christ. Without any regard to what we had done or would do, God in sovereign grace elected us to salvation (verse 13).

But divine election did not actually save us, and even though the Lord Jesus had provided a perfect redemption for us, His death of itself did not have any saving effects upon us while we were living in unbelief. The plan (election) was complete; the provision (Christ's death) was perfect; but the necessary condition for entering into the experience of salvation and of actually being justified before God needed implementation. We had to believe the gospel truth about the death,

Ephesians 2:1-3

"But God . . ." (Ephesians 2:4).

The gospel
content is
delineated in
I Corinthians
15:3,4.

Scripture
expressly states
that we
"obtained" faith;
we were not born
with it (II Peter
1:1).

John 6:44

Not one whom
the Father has
given to Christ
will be lost (John
6:39).

Romans 10:17

burial, and resurrection of Christ; we had to believe the truth about our natural corruption and the sole sufficiency of the Lord Jesus to save us.

Such belief was alien to our inborn depravity; and so the Holy Spirit, by His sanctifying grace, worked supernaturally in our minds, emotions, and wills to produce the necessary prerequisite of faith in us and then bring us to experience the salvation for which the Father had chosen us and the Son had redeemed us. Praise God for a salvation that is wholly of God from start to finish!

But how did the Holy Spirit bring us into the experience of salvation? The answer is clear—by calling us through the preaching of the gospel (verse 14). The divine calling is not simply a general invitation. The pastor, the teacher, or the evangelist issues gospel invitations, and men accept or reject the offer. But the divine call is an effectual summons from the Holy Spirit, who puts forth supernatural power and draws to Christ those whom He thus calls. No one has ever refused to obey the divine call, for the same Spirit who calls also produces a favorable response in those whom He summons.

If it were not for the Spirit's call, not a single soul would ever be saved in spite of the Father's plan and the Son's provision. Furthermore, not a single soul is ever saved without hearing or reading the Word of God. The Word of God is just as indispensable to salvation as faith is, for the Spirit's application of the Word generates faith in those whom God has elected to salvation.

These precious truths are calculated to inspire renewed steadfastness in the believer (verse 15). People who understand these truths aright have more zeal for evangelism, not less. They are more eager to preach the Word, for they know that this is God's means to rescue the perishing. They are more faithful in praying because they know that God alone can change the sinner's heart by transforming grace.

Because so much depends not upon human whims but upon the faithful transmission and propagation of the "traditions"—that is, the truths embodied in the doctrines of the apostles—the instructed believer puts a special emphasis upon the Holy Spirit's activity through the Word. For this reason Paul tells us that we must "hold" the Biblical teachings. By this he means that we should keep a firm grip upon them. It entails learning them, applying them, transmitting them, defending them, expounding them, cherishing them—in short, remaining faithful to them in word and deed.

Titus 1:9

Romans 1:16; I Corinthians 1:18; II Timothy 4:2

We lack no incentive for executing these imperatives. That love of God which prompted Him to give His Son as a sacrifice for us all prompts our steadfastness to the truth. As if this were not enough, God also gives us continual encouragement through "good hope" (verse 16). Our hope is not the futile, empty, and uncertain expectation of our contemporaries. It has a ring of certainty about it and cannot be frustrated because it rests upon Christ and His sure return.

I Peter 1:13

In verse 16 Paul uses the full title of the Lord Jesus Christ. Here is also a rare instance in which the name of the Son precedes that of the Father. It is also a bit unusual that Paul should direct his prayer to the Son; the customary mode of prayer is to address the Father in the name of the Son.

Stephen also prayed to Jesus (Acts 7:59,60).

Verse 17 adds its testimony to the essential oneness of the Father and Son. Although the subject of the verbs "comfort" and "stablish" is a compound noun and grammatically calls for plural verb agreement, Paul purposefully put the verbs in the singular number to show that the persons of the Godhead subsist as one God. Paul prayed that God the Father and God the Son will strengthen believers inwardly so that they will be enabled to hold forth the Word without doctrinal or practical deviation.

I Thessalonians 3:11 is another similar construction.

THE PRAYER OF PETITION
(II Thessalonians 3:1-5)

Paul did not think himself superior to the believers to whom he ministered. He considered them "brethren." Moreover, he valued their intercessory prayers on his behalf and urgently requested them to remember him before the throne of grace. He, too, needed spiritual stamina, but his primary concern was not for himself but for the success of the gospel. He longed for the Word of God to run freely, without opposition and obstacles (verse 1). This kind of circulation of the truth relates to prayer. Faithful prayer is as vital to the swift advance of the gospel as faithful preaching is.

Note Paul's chief concern in asking the Ephesians to pray for him (Ephesians 6:19,20).

Self-preservation for its own sake was not the aim of the apostle. He asked the Thessalonians to pray that God would rescue him from a particular situation which was not conducive to the spread of the gospel and which hindered the fulfillment of his apostolic calling. Fanatical Jews dogged his footsteps and threatened the gospel message. They were treacherous and fiendish, manifesting not only a deficiency of faith, but an utter destitution of it (verse 2). Wherever and whenever the true gospel of the grace of God is preached, a certain

Even adversities work toward the "furtherance of the gospel" (Philippians 1:12).

101

class of people will repudiate and resist it to their own destruction.

Nevertheless, the Lord is faithful, and His word will accomplish that for which He sends it (verse 3). He will not permit perverse men to get the upper hand. The activities of the evil one are always subject to God's control. The Christian takes refuge in the knowledge that God is faithful to establish His own people for the conflict and protect them in it.

Paul relied on the Lord so to work in the Thessalonians that they would do what he exhorted them (verse 4). Whatever we do must be done "in the Lord"—that is, in the power and inward impulse which comes to us from the Lord. We work in His strength and under His control. He has not left us to our natural powers or discretion. We trust Him for the perfecting of His own mighty work in our hearts and in the hearts of all who truly believe. Our confidence in and hope for others rests upon the Lord who has promised to cause them to stand (Romans 14:4).

Our love for God and our patient waiting for Christ are also subject of prayer (II Thessalonians 3:5). If we are to love God supremely, He must direct our hearts toward this end, and we are responsible to pray for this.

Paul longed to fulfill the purpose for which Christ laid hold of him in saving power (Philippians 3:12).

FOOD FOR THOUGHT

"The Bible doesn't say we should preach all the time, but it does say we should pray all the time."

—John R. Rice

NOW TEST YOUR KNOWLEDGE

True or False:

1. Divine election actually saves sinners. _____
2. Christians were saved in eternity past. _____
3. Salvation is two-sided: God's part and our part. _____
4. The call of the Spirit is a general invitation which does not necessarily result in salvation. _____
5. The Word of God plays only an incidental role in salvation. _____
6. The truths of election, predestination, etc., stifle evangelistic and missionary zeal. _____
7. God loves only a few people, and for that reason He elected only a few to be saved. _____

DEALING WITH CHURCH DISCIPLINE

13

LESSON SCRIPTURE
II Thessalonians 3:6-18

RELATED SCRIPTURE
Amos 3:3; Romans 16:17,18;
I John 1:7

LESSON AIM
To value diligence; to work
diligently.

LEARN BY HEART
"And if any man obey not our word
by this epistle, note that man, and
have no company with him, that he
may be ashamed"
(II Thessalonians 3:14).

EVERY DAY WITH THE WORD

Monday	Strengthened for work	Nehemiah 2:17-20
Tuesday	Opportunity for work	Nehemiah 3:1-32
Wednesday	A mind for work	Nehemiah 4:1-6
Thursday	Opposition to work	Nehemiah 4:7-23
Friday	Continuation of work	Nehemiah 5:14-19
Saturday	Finishing the work	Nehemiah 6:15-19
Sunday	Dedicating the work	Nehemiah 12:27-43

STUDENT'S NOTEBOOK

This column is for the student who desires additional study of the lesson theme.

LESSON PREPARATION

John Wesley traveled two hundred fifty thousand miles on horseback, averaging twenty miles a day for forty years; preached forty thousand sermons; produced four hundred books; knew ten languages. At eighty-three he was annoyed that he

Do you think it possible that this kind of activity is what Jesus referred to when He promised that

His followers would do greater works than He did (John 14:12)?

could not write more than fifteen hours a day without hurting his eyes, and at eighty-six he was ashamed he could not preach more than twice a day. He complained in his diary that there was an increasing tendency to lie in bed until 5:30 in the morning.

You wonder what Wesley would think of us if he were living today. We have come to think that the man who gets ahead is the one who knows best how to avoid hard work. We clamor for shorter working hours and better working conditions. We want more and more pay for doing less and less. We encourage the idle and pay reparations to rioters. People in many offices are being paid for eight hours a day and are working only four. We are a generation of pleasure seekers, shirkers of duty, and worshipers of leisure. The trend is not new. Paul had to deal with it at Thessalonica.

The lazy, ne'er-do-wells stirred up the riot at Thessalonica (Acts 17:5).

DISCIPLINING THE SHIRKERS
(II Thessalonians 3:6-12)

Paul advised the Ephesians that if they didn't want to suffer from financial need, they should work with their hands (4:28).

Lazy Christians are "disorderly" (verse 6). They are out of step with the Biblical principle which calls on every able-bodied man to earn his own living by honest labor. Even Adam in his unfallen estate had a God-appointed responsibility to work. His occupation consisted of dressing (cultivating) and keeping (protecting) the garden in which he dwelt. As a consequence of the fall of Adam the soil resisted his efforts, and man has had to toil by the sweat of his brow ever since. God sentenced the human race to a lifetime of hard labor not only as a punishment for sin but also as a measure to restrain his innate wickedness. Hardworking people do not have much time or energy to follow all the bents of their depravity.

Christians who work to support themselves have orders from the divine Commander-in-Chief through Paul to avoid the company of lazy brethren. The authority which Paul exercised in issuing such an ultimatum derived from Christ; he spoke as Christ's ambassador and in His stead. Disobedience to the command was a serious offense because it bore the stamp of the heavenly headquarters. No other option was available to the church. Obstinacy warrants church discipline. Until the slackers conform to order, the rest of the congregation must not make them feel welcome or give them the impression that they are members still in good standing.

II Corinthians 5:20

In dealing with truants from work, we do not want to go to extremes which Scripture does not sanction. To refuse to speak to the unruly or refuse them admittance to your home or business is going beyond anything that Paul had in mind when he instructed that we "withdraw" from them. Some well-meaning Christians have carried the principle so far as to refuse to ride in the same car with an erring brother. Others have refused to sit at the same table at home with members of their own immediate family who they considered were "disorderly."

III John 9:11

These severe measures are incompatible with Paul's instruction to do good to all men but especially to believers (Galatians 6:10). Certainly we would not treat unbelievers with more consideration than members of the household of faith, would we?

Paul did not mean that we should make an absolute and total break with idle saints, but he did want the church to act in such a way as to make the delinquents feel that a definite gap was making complete fellowship impossible while the offenders were sitting on their hands, letting their more industrious brethren support them.

Although he was a Roman citizen and articulate in the Greek language, Paul was never influenced by the Roman and Greek philosophy which regarded manual labor as fit only for slaves and degrading to freemen. Every Hebrew boy was instructed in a trade that could maintain him. Paul followed the Hebrew custom of occupying himself with menial tasks. He often had to fall back on tent-making to support himself. He set a good example of Christian industry to the Thessalonians, who had been considerably influenced, it seems, by Greek culture.

The Thessalonians knew that they should imitate Paul's example and give themselves to occupational pursuits (verse 7). They knew better than to abandon their secular employments supposedly to spend all their time witnessing to sinners and waiting for Jesus to come. If anyone had a legitimate reason for devoting all of his time to visitation, prayer, preaching, and personal counseling, it was the Apostle Paul. But no one could accuse him of being a loafer and living off the earnings of others while he wandered around the streets of Thessalonica all day "passing out tracts."

He did, however, accept love offerings from the Philippians while he worked in Thessalonica (Philippians 4:16).

He must have anticipated how the unsaved Jewish critics and the weaker Thessalonian converts would react if he accepted love offerings to support his ministry. The critics would have charged him with racketeering, and the babes in Christ would have followed Paul's example, expecting someone else to sponsor them in their retreat from work in favor of becoming itinerant beggars. Paul's conduct gave no one an opportunity to use the precedents which he set to their own advantage. Indeed, his life was a continual rebuke to idleness. He labored at tentmaking during the day from dawn 'til dusk and then carried

I Corinthians 4:9-17; II Corinthians 11:16-30

on the work of the gospel during the evening and into the night (verse 8).

We are not to imagine that Paul refused all hospitality while he labored in Thessalonica. Without a doubt, he had invitations to dinner and accepted them. What better place could he find to do the kind of personal evangelism he mentioned in I Thessalonians 2:11? But no one in the city could point a finger at Paul and say, "There goes the man that sponged off me and my family while he sat around for two weeks talking to people."

The laborer is worthy of his hire, and gospel work is labor that deserves remuneration. Those who preach the gospel should be able to make a decent living in their profession. Laying rewards up in Heaven won't feed the preacher's kids. Paul had the authority to demand support from his converts (II Thessalonica 3:9). But he refused to stand on his rights for fear that some would misunderstand his motives. In his decision to be independent of their financial help, he exhibited an unselfishness which all but a few laggards followed.

I Corinthians 9:7-18

The old adage, "No work, no supper," kept slothfulness at a minimum in Paul's day, and without a doubt an application of the same principle would get results today (verse 10). Able-bodied people who refuse to work when employment is available and who prefer to live on government handouts and welfare systems, because they can collect more money by spawning children than by working, might reevaluate their situation and go to work if their next meal depended on it.

Some people are poor through no fault of their own, and these have to be helped financially. Paul collected money to help the poor in Jerusalem (Romans 15:26; I Corinthians 16:1-3; see also Acts 11:27-29; Galatians 2:10).

Idle people will find something to do to escape boredom; usually they get into trouble (verse 11). At Thessalonica the dawdlers and the bummers found plenty to do by meddling in other people's affairs. They were overactive in monkey business but dullards in the business that counts most. Some had time for gossiping and criticism. Others idled away the hours by twiddling their thumbs and rocking in their easy chairs, waiting for Christ to break through the blue and initiate some action. Still others manifested an uncontrolled excitability which stimulated them to excessive talking and fluttering about in a kind of breathless effervescence.

Paul's orders were unmistakable: calm down and go about business as usual (verse 12). This is the will of "our Lord Jesus Christ." The doctrine of the Lord's return was never meant to send the child of God off on a hysterical tangent of irresponsibility. This truth should make us more honest and more diligent workers at the job which supports us while we witness in our off-business hours of God's saving grace and Christ's imminent return.

I Corinthians
7:20-24

DIRECTING THE WORKERS
(II Thessalonians 3:13-18)

Christians who stay at the job need to exercise a little forbearance toward Christians who are still wandering off course (verse 13). Our foremost desire should be to get them in line again so that they can become productive members of society as well as fruitful believers. Our fondest hope for them is that they will be assets rather than liabilities, and so we have to draw upon God's grace to muster the patience it requires to show them a better way. We may grow weary *in* the effort to reclaim them, but we cannot afford to

Love entertains
the best hopes
for others
(I Corinthians
13:7).

grow weary *of* the endeavor. The situation calls for unceasing attempts on the part of the spiritual Christian.

Both the "well doing" and the withdrawal are restorative in their intent (verse 14). Spot the man who refuses to work and stop fraternizing with him. The pain of loneliness will hurt him more than manual labor, and he will conform to Christian practice. If he senses that he is a marked man, he will feel so conspicuous and embarrassed that he will decide it is better to work than suffer the pangs of a tormented conscience. On the other hand, too drastic a treatment might alienate him or drive him to despond; therefore, he must be made to feel that we think of him as a brother even though we disapprove of his shiftless behavior (verse 15).

The church of Corinth took this action against a believer, and it produced good results (I Corinthians 5:5-13; II Corinthians 2:6-11; 7:10).

At some point in the last three verses Paul left off dictating the letter to his amanuensis and penned the concluding remarks in his own inimitable scrawl. It was a custom of the times which he adopted in order to assure the recipients of the letter that it was a genuine document. He continued the practice in the epistles to the Galatians (6:11), I Corinthians (16:21), and Colossians (4:18). The rest of his letters bore other proofs of their authenticity, and so he thought it unnecessary to write the last few comments himself.

If someone had forged Paul's name to a letter (II Thessalonians 2:2), he had good reason to take added precaution.

Verses 16 and 18 of II Thessalonians 3 consist of a benediction which takes the form of a supplication. Paul knew that only the Lord of peace could keep harmony in a church which exercised discipline; hence, he prayed that Christ would grant a settled calm where turbulence threatened to upset spiritual progress. He prayed that Christ by His spiritual presence would overrule all decisions of church discipline. At last he prayed that Christ would graciously deal with every single member of the church.

The grace of the Lord Jesus is the believer's only sufficiency for faithfully discharging the implications of the apostolic tradition. Grace can overcome inertia. Grace can control those who are high-strung. It can restrain those who are inclined to be meddlesome. Grace is adequate to strengthen our patience. It is all that we need and just what we need while we are waiting for the glorious appearing of our great God who is the Saviour, Jesus Christ.

FOOD FOR THOUGHT

"In works of labor, or of skill, I would be busy too, For Satan finds some mischief still for idle hands to do."

—Isaac Watts

NOW TEST YOUR KNOWLEDGE

Give short answers:

1. Where did work originate historically? _____
   _____

2. Why does the soil resist man's efforts? _____
   _____

3. What did Paul mean by "disorderly"? _____
   _____

4. Why did Paul do manual labor? _____
   _____

5. Who should work? _____
   _____

6. Why did some of the Thessalonians quit their jobs? _____

7. What should be our aim in dealing with lazy Christians? _____

8. How are the disorderly to be disciplined? _____
   _____

9. Why did Paul put the last few verses of the letter in his own handwriting? _____

10. What can the grace of the Lord Jesus do? _____
    _____